African Literature Today

A review
Edited by Eldred Durosimi Jones
Number 6: Poetry in Africa

T0339361

© Contributors 1973

All Rights Reserved. Except as permitted under current legislation
no part of this work may be photocopied, stored in a retrieval system,
published, performed in public, adapted, broadcast,
transmitted, recorded or reproduced in any form or by any means,
without the prior permission of the copyright owner

First published by Heinemann Educational Books 1973
Reprinted 1977, 1978, 1982

First published in the United States of America 1973
by Africana Publishing Corporation

James Currey, Woodbridge, Suffolk

ISBN 978 1 84701 119 0

Transferred to digital printing

James Currey is an imprint of Boydell & Brewer Ltd
PO Box 9, Woodbridge, Suffolk IP12 3DF, UK
and of Boydell & Brewer Inc.
668 Mt. Hope Avenue, Rochester NY 14620, USA
website: www.boydellandbrewer.com

This publication is printed on acid-free paper

Contents

Comments

Reviews

Corrigendum

We apologize for the consistent mis-spelling of Oyin Ogunba's name in ALT 4 and 5 – his article on 'The Traditional Content of the Plays of Wole Soyinka' appeared in No. 5. *Editor*

Editorial

Christopher Okigbo's presence on the African literary scene was tragically brief. With a little amendment his own lines characterize this brevity all too aptly:

> So brief [his] presence –
> match-flare in wind's breath . . .

Okigbo had in that passage lost his elusive goddess, the ideal for which he continually searched in his poetry. We have lost a rare poetic spirit who promised great things. To his memory, this number of *African Literature Today* is dedicated.

Two evaluations of Okigbo's work appear in this poetry number, which also contains studies of poetry from Algeria to South Africa. There has been a delay in its appearance because the whole edited copy was lost by the printers and had to be reassembled. All efforts to reach two of the original contributors, Marguerite McIntosh and Mary Van der Water failed, and their articles have therefore not appeared. The loss of Miss McIntosh's contribution is particularly regretted since it was to have been the third on Okigbo's poetry.

It has unfortunately become necessary to say that unsolicited articles will not be returned unless sufficient international posting coupons are sent for the purpose. This is not intended as a discouragement to intending contributors but it must be stated that it is getting increasingly difficult to fit all the unsolicited articles we receive into our single annual number.

ELDRED D. JONES

ARTICLES

Okigbo's Portrait of the Artist as a Sunbird: A Reading of 'Heavensgate' (1962)

D. S. Izevbaye

1

HEAVENSGATE AND LABYRINTHS

The year 1971 saw the publication by Heinemann Educational Books of *Labyrinths with Path of Thunder*, a collection which is in one respect the final edition of Okigbo's work although, because of the omission of the Canzones and at least two of the later poems, its finality consists not in completeness but in saving editors of Okigbo's poems the trouble of having to decide what the poet actually wrote or intended to write. An additional value of this collection is the poet's introductory interpretation or, as interpretations are never known to be final, a description of the design of the poems which should become the basis of future interpretations. By thus providing the reader with an outline map of *Labyrinths*, Okigbo has cleared some of the paths to his poetic experience and has probably helped to arrest the growing tendency to regard the experience as something that is not available to the reader. This view of the poems as an impenetrable territory has been encouraged by reports of Okigbo's early view of poetry as a type of cult from which the uninitiated is excluded and by the cautious critical explications – often necessarily cautious, admittedly – in which the critic and the reader are unmasked as intruders. This impression of a closed world has been a potential inhibition to response, and the poet has thrown down this psychological barrier by offering the elucidations in *Labyrinths*.

The poetry remains a genuinely difficult one by itself, of course. To be **1** able to find their way through the labyrinths of allusions to personal myths and forgotten cultures many readers will have to rely on the thread of meaning provided in the introduction and the notes. However, this change in respect of the poet's attitude to the reader reflects the difference between *Labyrinths* and the discrete earlier versions of Okigbo's poetry. In the earlier versions the uninitiated reader is understandably excluded from the poetic experience because the poet is himself still being initiated. *Labyrinths* follows the path of exploration or inquiry leading to discovery or revelation. With the poet's discovery of the true pattern of his initiation the reader can now be taken through the different stages until he too is finally admitted into the sanctuary. Each of the earlier sequences is incomplete by itself because it is only an investigation of the poet's partial glimpse of an experience, and only the complete group of sequences can provide a reliable blueprint from which a reader might reconstruct the poetic experience. The earlier poems are not then the true gateways; or if they are gateways they often lead to blind alleys, though they are useful as reflections of the poet's own wanderings and losses of direction before the surer path of his pilgrimage is revealed in the continuity of *Labyrinths*.

The revisions which result in *Labyrinths* are, like most revisions, necessary for a clearer and more accurate statement of the poet's experience. Nevertheless the earlier poems are of value because they tell a fairly accurate story of the process of composition. An interpretation of the revisions shows that in addition to the need for an efficient performance the final version required the tailoring of the old poems in order to fit the new need. One of the most important changes in *Labyrinths* is the cutting out of 'Transition' from *Heavensgate*. Without necessarily committing oneself to a fallacy by describing as the poet's intention what is really an effect of the final revision, one may justify the excision of 'Transition' by arguing that its triumphant tone is not quite consistent with the humble and exploratory spirit of *Heavensgate*, and that this tone is contradicted, in 'Siren Limits', by the poet's use of the image of the shrub or the low growth which confesses a striving towards maturity rather than claim a full maturing of poetic powers. However if there is something inconsistent about the claims of 'Transition' in the light of the actual performance of *Heavensgate* this section of the poem is itself less out of place in the original sequence than it would have been in *Labyrinths* within which the *Heavensgate* sequence itself is mainly an introduction or a prelude. In other words it was necessary to eliminate an end which has turned out to be a true end no longer.

If the 1962 version of the sequence would not fit into *Labyrinths* without modification it nevertheless has its own completeness, and the different sections have their justification for being in the poem, although the question that has most frequently been raised is that of the relevance of the parts.

The organic unity of Okigbo's poems should seem a fairly commonplace idea by now, since it was emphasized in the earliest as well as in the most recent comments on the poetry – in Anozie's review[1] as well as in Okigbo's introduction. But although this underlying principle of composition has long been recognized it has not always been accepted as generally applicable to all the poems. For example, 'Newcomer', the fifth movement of *Heavens-gate*, is sometimes seen as separate from the rest of the poem because its sections were originally composed as separate poems and at different times.[2]

The ground for such a doubt is of course Okigbo's method of com-position which creates the impression that each poem is an assemblage that may be dismantled and re-assigned to the various sources, like Tutuola's Complete Gentleman. For example, it seems as if some of the units is an Okigbo sequence can comfortably be moved to other positions especially when, because of the omission of existing parts or the addition of others, a new relationship is created between the parts which makes it necessary to re-examine the meaning conveyed. Such a reassignment is evident in both *Modern Poetry from Africa* (1963) and *Labyrinths* where 'Bridge' is moved from its place in the middle of *Heavensgate* to the end in order to link the sequence with *Limits*. A discussion of Okigbo's poems therefore should assume the reader's acceptance of the essential looseness of structure arising from this method of composition. In this respect the sequences have a kinship with primitive epics because the poems appear to be a series of predetermined *forms* which attract independent poetic compositions to themselves. An important factor in the composition of extended traditional poems, especially primitive epics, is the fact that poems originally created as separate compositions cease to be considered independent units after they have been organized into larger units. The process of composition appears to be the adoption of a conventional, but fairly loose, structure within which individual experiences may establish a logical relationship with one another. The most favoured structures are usually those con-nected with social institutions or with religious or ritual performance. The relevance of this to a discussion of *Heavensgate* is obvious. The poem deals with the personal experiences of the hero. Its theme is the growth of a poet's mind. To the extent that the poem has a biographical – or auto-biographical – structure, each of its movements represents the moments of crisis in the hero's life. So it is possible to regard any equivalent struc-ture – like the basic stages of a man's life, Childhood, Adolescence, and Maturity – as the scaffolding around which the poem is constructed. The period of composition notwithstanding, poems about various experiences fit into the various stages whether as crises, or as the cause or the resolution of crises. The act of creation may thus be seen to consist mainly in a **3** structural arrangement which makes each unit of the poem subordinate to, and a functional part of, the overall organization.

This emphasis on organization also makes it necessary to adopt a more flexible view of originality with regard to the problem of the literary influences or borrowings in the poems. For the purpose of this essay it is useful to make a distinction between literary echoes and literary borrowings. Literary echoes are resonances of an original, and to get a full experience of the poem the reader requires some knowledge of the original. And although such a poem might have an independent existence, like *The Waste Land*, the poems which it echoes are often part of the aesthetic experience of the poem, since the echoes are adaptations of an accepted context the knowledge of which, while not being essential, is invariably enriching.

In literary borrowing, on the other hand, knowledge of the original context contributes little or nothing to the experience of the new poem. It might in fact be a hindrance to proper critical response. The borrowed phrase or sentence is often used with little regard for its source, as in some of Okigbo's poems where not much is gained from a knowledge of the original poem. For usually Okigbo's interest in his borrowings seems limited to the beauty and the utility of the phrase itself, and the 'meaning' or 'experience' of the poem is often controlled by its immediate context.[3] This is mostly true even when, as in the title *Heavensgate*, the borrowed word affects the reader's response in the right direction before the context has had a chance to do its work. The discussion which follows is based on the text of 1962. The chart at the end of the essay indicates what sections of *Heavensgate* are available in revised form in *Labyrinths*.

2

HYMNS AT HEAVENSGATE

The title *Heavensgate* appears to be a word abstracted from a context, and the context that readily suggests itself is Shakespeare's twenty-ninth sonnet where the bard is lifted from a mood of depression to sing 'hymns at heaven's gate' by the thought of love.[4] There is the same movement from despair to elation in the two poems. In both cases the central symbol is a singing bird. Even the image of the importunate outcast at the ears of deaf heaven in the sonnet seems reflected in the prodigal's apparent return to a starting point after an abortive attempt at entry. But it is not essential to see the title as a literary echo in order to notice that the sunbird is the central image of the poem, or that the whole poem is conceived as a musical form in which much value is attached to the interplay of sounds.

4   The conception of the poem as musical form is apparent in the opening

invocation which is used as a prelude to introduce the main motif of the piece. This function is more apparent in the anthology by Moore and Beier where the adopted title 'Overture' provides an apt musical analogy by emphasizing the introductory function of the invocation as well as describing the relationship between the suppliant and the goddess. Since the first movement, 'Passage', deals with the period of passage from boyhood to manhood, the prelude is appropriately a physical dramatization of an attempted entry into a spiritual or aesthetic state. The central movements of the poem are concerned with such attempts in the present time. The events of the present are explained in the past, which is the period dealt with by the first two movements, 'Passage' and 'Initiation'. 'Transition', which is the coda to the whole sequence, anticipates the hero's passage into a future state, a state which is never really achieved in Okigbo's poetry except in *Distances*. Although 'Transition' foretells a state which *Distances* enacts, the vision which it presents – the uninhibited release of unlimited song – is not achieved in the poem itself, as is made clear in the structure of *Heavensgate*. In fact the effective mood of Okigbo's first two sequences is not fulfilment but anticipation. So that even by the end of 'Siren Limits' the resolution of the crisis is deferred to future time:

> When you have finished
> & done up my stitches,
> Wake me near the altar,
> & this poem will be finished . . .

WHEN WE WERE GREAT BOYS

'Passage' as a whole deals with the hero's early childhood responses to experience. But although there is an attempt, in 'Passage (ii)', to recapture childhood experience by reproducing sounds mimicked by the boys, both 'Passage' and 'Initiation' deal with experience in retrospect. Although 'the young bird at the passage' is the observer of the spectacle in 'Passage (i)' (probably the onset of a thunderstorm), it is the mind of the mature artist which now interprets this scenery as a reproduction of the creation scene, and takes us back to that period 'when we were great boys' and 'sang words after the birds'.

This second section is central to the first two movements of the poem because of the way it uses the symbols of bird and light establishes their significance for the rest of the poem. After the associations built up by this section, light and bird would together herald the lyric impulse in both *Heavensgate* and *Limits*.

Meanwhile 'Passage (iii)' picks up the image of the bird with which the preceding section closes, and with it defines and enlarges the theme of creation with which the first section opens. It does this by presenting the 5 two major forms which the boys' introduction into the act of creation has taken. These are represented as at play at the blacksmiths' forge, and at work with the teacher at school. Since these introductions to experience take the form of response, there is possibly a third situation in which it occurs – that of worship in church. But this is not introduced until later.

The emphasis on response as the main factor in the boys' formative period shows that in 'Passage (ii)' the boys are passing through a period of pupilage. Those gifts which are to survive into their adult life are already in evidence here – the fascination which song holds for them is evident in their imitation of bird sounds – 'kratosbiate'. There is also the identification of these sounds with other fascinating sounds the children are made to imitate at school, as in their dutiful response to the sing-song recitation of their teacher, 'Etru bo pi a lo a she . . .'[5] The metonymy, 'white buck and helmet', shows the teacher himself as seen through childhood eyes. As if to show that both experiences are really part of the same experience in spite of their separate locations at school and at play, the flames of the forge become metaphor for the shaping influence of school where boys are pulled through innocence, and the smith's workshop becomes a new setting for learning. The boys show a preference for the latter setting, since the symbols of school influence are consigned to the flames. That is why 'burn' is possibly ambiguous in the following extract:

> And we would respond,
> great boys of child–innocence,
> and in the flames burn
> > white buck and helmet
> that had pulled us through innocence. . . .

The lines would normally be read to mean, 'we would burn white buck and helmet in the flames'; but it could also imply, 'we would burn [be shaped] in the flames'.

If religion does not feature as an important influence in those two sections it sounds the dominant note in the rest of 'Passage' and 'Initiation', and helps to define the unpleasant experiences which force the prodigal to accept the necessity for homecoming. In 'Passage (ii)' the real centre of the Christian procession is the overwhelming bewilderment which the poet feels on arriving at a crossroads or a turning point in his development. This mood is achieved through an emphasis on the solemnity and on the mourning colour which marks the procession and which identifies the poet's mood with the traditional feeling of loss and alienation associated with mournings. The fragments of melody, the appeal to a personal saint, 'Anna of the panel oblongs', and the refuge in the cornfields among the

6 wild music of the winds complete the mourner's feeling of a broken emo-

tional anchor. Thus begins the prodigal's progress from separation through bewilderment and alienation which are the preludes to his renunciation of the Christian religion.

'Passage (iii)' outlines the hero's initial objections to Christianity; its foreign origin is emphasized in the drama of the seven-league boots striding over distant seas and deserts; its oppressiveness is implied in the designation of Leidan as 'archtyrant of the holy sea' (an obvious pun); and the aversion which he feels for Christian ritual and its reward is present in the report on the fate of people like Paul, who, after conversion, become subjected to the:

> smell of rank olive oil
> on foreheads,
> vision of the hot bath of heaven
> among reedy spaces.

OF POETRY, RELIGION, AND SIN

Having had a foretaste of various forms of experience in 'Passage' (play, education, religion), the poet recalls, in 'Initiation', his formal introduction into the adult world of religion, poetry, and sex. His introduction to the first takes the form of a ritual initiation, but his introduction to the other two areas of experience occurs as a form of discovery. As might have been anticipated in the previous section, the prodigal's first significant experience of religion takes the form of a painful initiation which he sees rather resentfully as a branding that has the claims of a legal agreement:

> Scar of the crucifix
> over the breast
> by red blade inflicted
> by red-hot blade on right breast
> witnesseth

The pain itself is not the cause but the consequence of his resentment. The cause stems from his conception that ideally, the initiated should be

> Elemental, united in vision
> of present and future,
> the pure line, whose innocence
> denies inhibitions.

Instead of this promised transformation the initiated ones turn out to be worthless or corrupt adherents whom the poet has arranged in categories which include lifeless morons, fanatics, and self-seekers. This perversion of good intentions is imputed to cultural differences. Maybe that is why the 7 hero seeks refuge in the memory of a childhood experience in the third section.

The second and central theme of the poem is presented in 'Initiation (iii) and (iv)'. 'Initiation (iii)' returns us the poet's childhood. The theme is music making, with Jadum the minstrel singing cautionary songs from the fairyland of youth till late into the night. The opening lines are a suggestion that Jadum got his name from the sound of his music, 'JAM JAM DUM DUM'. The emphasis is not so much on his madness as on the music he makes. The power of his minstrelsy over the childish listener is the theme of the section. And yet the fact of his madness is important too, for the identification of poetry with madness is also the theme of 'Newcomer (ii)' where the hero is 'mad with the same madness as the / moon and my neighbour'.

FOR POETS ONLY
'Initiation (iv)' focuses attention directly on the art of poetry by formulating a poetic. The formulation takes the form of a dialogue with 'upandru'. The first item defines Okigbo's technique, his delight in mystifying the reader with recondite references. Obscurity is a technique for hiding the poet's thoughts: 'Screen your bedchamber thoughts / with sunglasses'. The second item, the view that only poets may penetrate beyond this mask, might explain why, as was once reported, Okigbo claimed, 'I don't read my poetry to non-poets':[6]

> who could jump your eye
> your mind-window?
>
> And I said:
> The prophet only,
> The poet.

The bedchamber is introduced in the fifth section where the poet screens his thoughts with a riddle. In this introduction of the third theme, the sexual, the poet rejects the Christian call of 'Initiation (i)' for a 'life without sin'. In his conviction that freedom from lust can come only through indulgence the prodigal has found a philosophy to live by. By this rejection of an alien religion and the adoption of poetry and of a personal code of existence, the prodigal-poet considers his initiation into a new personal world complete, and feels ready for union with Watermaid. 'Bridge' represents this stage of the anticipation of her influence.

THE HOMECOMING
The desired union with Watermaid is however not consummated in the third movement. There is a stage missing in the ritual of the prodigal's

return, and that is, an identification of the source to which he is returning, and a performance of the requirements for readmission. 'Initiation' has turned out a misleading experience. What he describes in the first section is merely an abortive initiation; and although he achieves something in the first two sections by completing the renunciation of his prostituted allegiance, he does not go further than an examination and a discovery of his own purposes in the last two sections. In fact no adequate preparation for the meeting with Watermaid has taken place. That is why, as the poet discovers, 'Bridge' has been a premature stage in his homecoming. So although the goddess responds to the prodigal's cry, the revelation is too evanescent to be of permanent value to the poet who now watches the loss of the harvest:

> So brief her presence –
> match-flare in wind's breath –
> so brief with mirrors around me.
>
> Downward . . .
> the waves distil her:
> gold crop
> sinking ungathered.

The lament in 'Watermaid (iii)' involves not merely alienation but also a loss of the expected harvest. In 'Watermaid (iv)', for example the departure of the stars is used not only as a backdrop to the isolation of the poet, it is also a reference to 'Watermaid (i)' in which poetic blessing is expected when the eyes of the prodigal 'upward to heaven shoot / where stars will fall from'. That is why the prodigal-poet strives to recapture the fleeting strains of poetic inspiration in a passage that anticipates the second movement of *Limits*:

> Stretch, stretch, O antennae,
> to clutch at this hour,
>
> fulfilling each moment in a
> broken monody.

The reason for the failure to achieve full union with Watermaid has been revealed earlier where the suppliant hid the secret in beach sand. The goddess has discovered that the candidate for initiation is ritually unclean and therefore unfit for her presence. All he has done is to go through an adapted form of Christian confession without using a priest – an unsuitable ritual, for Watermaid is unambiguously presented as 'native' – in a renunciation of the Christian experience. That is why, in spite of being from the **9** sea, she is 'Watermaid of the salt emptiness'. Salt water has become distasteful because of its supposed association with the baptismal rites of primitive Christianity:

> so comes John the Baptist
> with bowl of salt water

Since Watermaid is not a Christian goddess we may assume that she belongs mainly to a non-Christian, even pre-Christian, religion or community.

It follows, then, that the particular defilement we are concerned with is non-Christian and even non-ethical, and that the state of impurity should not be linked with the prodigal's rejection of Christian insistence on continence in the 'Initiation' movement. In fact the recurrence of the he-goat-on-heat motif in *Limits* reinforces this view that the uncleanliness which drove Watermaid away from contact with pollution, and makes the 'Lustra' movement of *Heavensgate* necessary, is a ceremonial rather than an ethical or moral purification. Ritual offering is necessary only because the poet-hero has been a prodigal and is therefore technically a stranger requiring ritual cleansing before being readmitted into communion with his goddess.

It is this purification feast that is variously celebrated in the three parts of 'Lustra': first the traditionally prescribed objects of purification in the first part; then the spirit's hopeful ascent towards acceptance to an accompaniment of ceremonial drums and cannons in the second part; finally, the vegetable and chalk that are offered in the third part as an act of penitence to complete the requirement partially fulfilled by the performances in the earlier sections. Although the offerings are all traditional ones, they possess the attributes of moistness and whiteness which have been associated with the goddess. Also like the goddess, the attitude is 'native'. It will be noticed that in the line, 'whitewashed in the moondew', a common Christian moral attitude has been purged from the word, 'whitewash', which is now reinvested with a non-Western, traditional ritual meaning. We may assume that his renunciation is final at this stage.

In the third section the poet adopts the underlying faith of the religion from which he is a refugee; the rejection of the source of the faith is explicit in the attitude of 'After the argument in heaven'. The doctrine has relevance for the prodigal because it provides reassurance in the analogy drawn with the Christian belief in the Second Coming – the reappearance of his Watermaid, after the fulfilment of the lustral requirements.

It is this expected second coming of Watermaid which makes the fifth movement, 'Newcomer', a necessary conclusion for *Heavensgate*. Having **10** lost his first opportunity to achieve communion with Mother Idoto, it is only in 'Newcomer' that the poet gets another opportunity to hold himself open to poetic inspiration from his native muse, after his blunder in the 'Watermaid' movement. Although 'Newcomer' suffers from repetition in the context of the poem since the first two sections take the reader over some old ground, on the whole it moves us a step further towards the close of the hero's development. For example, in the opening lines the peals of the angelus recall the prodigal's state of exile, and the involuntary sign of the cross which accompanies these bells becomes transformed into a gesture of defiance against the usual response. It also serves him as a protective mask to insulate his new individuality from being swamped by communal values:

> Mask over my face –
>
> my own mask
> not ancestral –

Thus, the internalized allegiance which makes it irresistible for the Christian to respond spontaneously at the sight or sound of Christian symbols is tested against the hero's new-found identity. The appeal to the personal 'Saint', Anna, for succour is a desperate step which he takes because he is threatened by the danger of succumbing to the Christian call to worship.

'Newcomer (ii)', by no means the happiest section, repeats the theme of identity just presented in the first section. It is dedicated to a kindred spirit. Both 'spirits' are isolated from the generality of men by their madness – for what is madness but a deviation from commonly-accepted norms of behaviour. It is this common 'insanity' of creative spirits which unites the hero and Peter Thomas with Jadum, the mad minstrel of 'Initiation (iii)'.

The final section of 'Newcomer' is also a dedicatory piece: 'For Georgette', written as a kind of nativity poem. Although, like the section dedicated to Peter Thomas, this piece was originally occasional, it finds a logical context in *Heavensgate*. Its burden is the final arrival of the much-longed-for inspiration which gave the whole of the *Heavensgate* sequence its exploratory structure and the strongly expectant tone first dictated by the 'Watchman for the watchword' in the overture. But this section is not a description of the composition of *Heavensgate*, as Anozie pointed out in the review. It only heralds the arrival of poetic inspiration, for *Heavensgate* is an account of its own uncompleted quest only, and the reader is left at that point of elated expectancy just as inspiration descends – a point just one stage ahead of 'Watermaid (i)', and one behind 'Watermaid (ii)'. A suitable setting to have the muse delivered has been created in 'May', 'green', and 'garden'. The 'synthetic welcome' suits the experimentation **11** with words and form which gets the poet ready to welcome inspiration when it arrives.

We are now ready for the actual manifestation of the poetic impulse. The blinded heron of 'Transition' proclaims the birth of song, and anticipates the fulfilment of the goal towards which *Heavensgate* has been developing. The poem closes by the use of images with which the poet initially dramatized the problems of creation. The heron is of course the 'sunbird' of 'Passage' now developed into a mature bird, and it is to become the talkative weaver-bird of *Siren Limits*. We are also to meet him in *Fragments out of the Deluge* as the martyred songster who arose, like the phoenix from its ashes, to hymn new songs of its own immortality.

The song of *Heavensgate* ends as darkness descends over the setting, a contrast with the sunrise scene of the opening movement. This is achieved by a tempering of the dominant colours of the poem – transparency replaces the brilliant white of 'Watermaid', and soft leaf green replaces the bright, violent colours of the creation scene – i.e. the red, violet and orange of 'Passage (i)'. Natural phenomena, too, undergo this change: the moon goes under the sea – and it will be remembered that in 'Newcomer (ii)' the moon is the source of madness and inspiration, and that the sea is the home of Watermaid, goddess of inspiration. When the song is over, the inspirer goes home to rest, leaving the poet spent but sane; leaving only the shade to cloud the play of colour and sound.

And we have to wait until *Limits* when the poet is seized in a new poetic frenzy, his tongue having been liberated after appropriate purification.

NOTES

1. S. O. Anozie, 'Okigbo's *Heavensgate*, a study of Art as Ritual', *Ibadan*, No. 15 (March 1963), p. 11.
2. O. R. Dathorne, 'Ritual and ceremony in Okigbo's Poetry', *Journal of Commonwealth Literature*, No. 5 (July 1968), p. 84.
3. Some would deny that there is any such contextual control of meaning. E.g., Ali Mazrui argues that Okigbo's poetry 'leaves the reader no room for being *wrong* in his interpretation'. 'Abstract Art and African Tradition', *Zuka*, No. 1 (September 1967), p. 47.
4. Note the reference also in *Cymbeline*, Act II, Scene 3: 'Hark! Hark! the lark at heaven's gate sings.'
5. According to Okigbo himself, this line is a rendering of a child's phonetic variation on the nursery rhyme, 'Little Bo Peep'. 'Death of Christopher Okigbo', *Transition*, No. 33 (October/November 1967), p. 18. The poet eliminates the nostalgia of this lost paradise by leaving the section out of the *Labyrinths* version.
6. Bloke Modisane, 'The Literary Scramble for Africa', *West Africa* (30 June 1962), p. 176.

Heavensgate, Mbari, 1962		*Labyrinths,* Heinemann, 1971	
Idoto [Overture]		I The Passage (3 sections)	
I Passage	(i)	p. 3	
	(ii)	p. 4	
	(iii)	—	
	(iv)	p. 5	
		—	
II Initiation		II Initiations (3 sections)	
	(i) ⎱		
	(ii) ⎰	pp. 6–7	
	(iii)	p. 8	
	(iv) ⎱		
	(v) ⎰	p. 9	
Bridge		[p. 19 (Newcomer)]	
III Watermaid		III Watermaid (4 sections)	
	(i)	p. 10	
	(ii)	p. 11	
	(iii)	p. 12	
	(iv)	p. 13	
IV Lustra		IV Lustra (3 sections)	
	(i)	p. 14	
	(ii)	p. 16	
	(iii)	p. 15	
V Newcomer		V Newcomer (3 sections)	
	(i)	p. 17	
	(ii)	—	
	(iii)	p. 18	
Transition		– (replaced by what used to be 'Bridge')	

Defence of Culture in the Poetry of Christopher Okigbo

Romanus Egudu

> Before you, mother Idoto,
>   naked I stand,
> Before your watery presence,
>   a prodigal,
> Leaning on an oilbean,
> Lost in your legend . . .

INTRODUCTION

One of the worst effects of colonialism and colonial evangelization in West Africa is the suppression of the indigenous West African culture in general and the indigenous religious worship in particular. The efforts of the early Christian missionaries were directed at estranging the natives from their indigenous religion and 'planting' them in the imported Christian religion. Christopher Okigbo sees himself as a prodigal who has left this home religion for the foreign one. And at a moment of mature realization he returns to his original religion to revive and preserve the indigenous system of worship. This accounts for the satirical attitude to Christianity in his poetry and for his sincere and devoted participation in the traditional religious worship.

In literary culture also, Okigbo experiences some inhibition, which is a kind of hang-over from colonialism. He has to struggle against odds to make a success of writing poetry, for the critics are ever ready with their paternalistic pieces of prohibitive advice which created 'banks of reeds' and 'mountains of broken bottles' for the young African poet. Thus throughout Okigbo's poems, besides the themes of religious suppression, anti-Christianity, and religious revival, that of literary struggle is quite glaring.

SUPPRESSION OF INDIGENOUS RELIGION

Early in *Heavensgate* ('Passage (i)'),[1] Okigbo strikes a sad note. It is a note of mourning a dead mother. Like a 'Sunbird' the protagonist of the poem

sings a song of woe:

Me to the orangery
solitude invites,
a wagtail, to tell
the tangled-wood-tale;
a sunbird, to mourn
a mother on a spray.

To the poet the mother represents the indigenous culture. She is the same mother Idoto addressed in the poem 'Idoto', who is a river-goddess. And the poet's indigenous religion centres on the worship of this goddess. This goddess (mother) is, as it were, dead (i.e. suppressed by the Christian religion) and the poet is mourning her.

The loss of the indigenous religion is a serious loss, for it implies the loss of 'innocence'. Thus in the second part of 'Passage' the poet responded to the song of the sunbird during his period of his 'innocence' and that was before 'white buck and helmet' representing Christian missionaries 'pulled us through innocence'.

Christianity has waged a terrible war against the indigenous gods. Historically, this is quite true. Sir Alan Burns has this to say in this connection:

Although the change is slow, it is unquestionable that paganism is gradually yielding in Nigeria to the influence of Islam and Christianity, partly perhaps on account of the social and political advantages of these religions.[2]

In the 1940s, even a non-missionary colonialist like Mr Chadwick, who was then in charge of Udi Division, once swooped upon the village gods in the Division. He desecrated them and asked their priests to offer them the kind of sacrifice which was forbidden by the indigenous religious law. When the priests refused, he had them imprisoned.

Okigbo's poetry reflects this kind of situation. *Limits* VII[3] shows Flannagan (a Catholic Missionary) preaching 'the Pope's message':

To sow the fireseed among grasses,
and lo,
To keep it till it burns out. . . .

The message is to the effect of destruction; and there is the implication that it will be effective, for when fire is set to grass, the grass will naturally be burnt clear.

In *Limits* IX the enemies of the indigenous gods are shown in action. These are the Christian missionaries or their agents. They first kill the 'sunbird' which is sacred to the gods, and then, entering the forest, find **15** the twin-gods living there. The silence which pervades the forest and which is 'within me' signifies the sorrow that will arise from the vandalism of the invading 'beasts'. These 'beasts' – the enemies of the gods – are cursing: 'Malisons, malisons . . .' – 'malison' being a sort of malediction. 'Bombax' helps to characterize the enemies. The image of climbing the 'bombax' very exquisitely externalizes the impulse of pride and pomposity of the Christian-enemies of the indigenous gods. They are birds of prey who possess 'talons' which 'they drew out of their scabbard', and 'beaks' also which 'they sharpened'. Thus equipped, they fall 'upon the twin-gods of Irkalla'. Like the soldiers who cast lots on the garment of Christ after crucifying him, the despoilers of Okigbo's 'twin-gods' divide among them the gods' 'ornaments', 'beads', 'carapace', and 'shell'. The evocation of the Christian image (death of Christ) is a variation of the technique of juxtaposing Christian and indigenous images, which Ulli Beier has noted.[4] Besides, in this very incident of the killing of the twin-gods the Christian and the pagan meet together. The fertility ritual in which a god is killed or hanged – an old pagan practice[5] – is reflected by Okigbo, though his context shows an antagonistic rather than a religious purpose.

The 'calamity' does not end with the killing of the gods; it is protracted into complete desecration – 'the gods lie in a state / without the long-drum', and unsung; they lie outside the 'Shrinehouse', mouldy and forgotten. And pathetically, almost ironically, the poet points out a platitude upon which he could lean for consolation:

> Gods grow out,
> abandoned;
> And so do they. . . .

Limits X takes us back to the beginning of *Limits* IX, and shows how the 'Sunbird' was killed and brings the process of the sacrilegious destruction to a conclusion The sunbird sings again, but this time from 'the *Limits* of the dream'. It sings of Guernica

> On whose canvas of blood,
> The newspring-slits of his tongue
> cling to glue . . .
> & the cancelling out is complete.

Thus with the killing of the 'twin-gods' and the 'Sunbird' which is sacred to them and which indeed symbolizes their priest, then, of course, the process of the suppression of the indigenous religion is complete.

Another poem by Okigbo handles this theme in a more general way. 'Lament of the Drums'[6] (the second part of *Silences*) deals with oppression, captivity and suffering, robbery of others' right and freedom, and the resultant desolation. After the oppressive experiences, 'nothing remains' except the 'broken tin-gods whose / Vision is dissolved' (Section III). Here as in *Limits* the sad note is on destroyed gods.

ANTI-CATHOLICISM

Christopher Okigbo's reaction to the Christianity that has suppressed his home religion and its gods is that of contempt and sharp criticism. For Christianity has done him two wrongs. First, it has estranged him from his indigenous system of worship for some period of his life; and secondly it has nothing reasonable to offer him instead. Because of his sad experiences in the Catholic religion, he satirizes the Catholic Church in his poems.

In 'Passage (iv)' (*Heavensgate*) we hear of the 'bye laws thereto appended / by Leidan / archtyrant of the holy sea'. 'Bye laws' may refer to the Ten Commandments or the regulations of the Catholic Church, or to both. 'Leidan' is certainly a Catholic priest (or bishop), for he represents the 'holy sea' (a parody of Holy See), and he is 'archtyrant'. We know that this is so because 'Leidan' has the power to forgive sins, and the 'forgiveness' is given 'upon the waters of the genesis / by Leidan'. In the same poem there is also a contemptuous reference to the Catholic practice of anointing the foreheads during the administration of such sacraments as Baptism, Confirmation, Extreme Unction, etc. Of this the poet says:

> Smell of rank olive oil
> on foreheads,
> vision of the hot bath of heaven
> among reedy spaces.

It is in 'Initiation' in *Heavensgate* that the satire reaches a climax. In 'Initiation (i)' we learn that the poet (or protagonist) was indoctrinated by Kepkanly (a nickname for a catechist) from whom he received the 'mystery' 'upon waters of the genesis'. 'Scar of the crucifix' in this poem is a sign or 'witness' of the mystery of baptism which the poet received, for this 'Scar of the crucifix / over the breast' 'witnesseth' the 'mystery which, I initiate, / received newly naked / upon waters of the genesis. . . .' The interpretation given to this passage by Paul Theroux and O. R. Dathorne therefore seems to me to be wrong. For they said that it signifies that the poet is crucified like Christ.[7] The important point is that the 'scar' is not a pleasant thing. 'Scar' results from the wound inflicted on the poet by baptism; so to him the Catholic baptism has been an ugly experience.

We next hear of John the Baptist who preached the 'gambit', and this is 'life without sin, without/life', and one is not expected to make 'decisions' **17** about accepting it. This is the Catholic theory of faith – believing without doubting what God has revealed. 'Life . . . without life' sounds satirical. It commands life without carnal enjoyments, and as we shall see in section (v) of 'Initiation', it seems impossible to the poet.

The ridicule continues in the representation of the Church organization in terms of mathematical symbols:

> Square yields the moron,
> fanatics and priests and popes,
> organizing secretaries and
> party managers; better still,
>
> the rhombus – brothers and
> deacons and liberal politicians and
>   selfish selfseekers and all
> who are good doing nothing at all;
>
> the quadrangle, the rest,
> me and you. . . .

In the first two stanzas above, the poet has lumped the clergy and politicians together, implying that both groups are equally corrupt, deceitful, and selfish. It should be noted that here he is attacking the management of religion and politics, not religion *per se* as an institution. After all he is all the time defending his own indigenous religion against foreign corruption and desecration. He accepts that the 'Mystery' (of religion) would be a witness to the 'red-hot blade on right breast' . . . 'scar of the crucifix' if only there were not the 'errors of the rendering'. In other words, to him, the rulers of the Church have misinterpreted the religion of Christ.

In sections (iii), (iv) and (v) the poet gets into the area of church preaching, which is all in the form of prohibition: not to 'wander in speargrass' in the dark; not to 'Listen to a keyhole' – (eavesdropping?) (iii). To the poet these warnings were meaningless, commonplace and unnecessary, and that is why he thinks that:

> . . . there are here
> the errors of the rendering

When it is realized that 'Jadum' who issued these warnings was a madman who lived in Aguata County of Awka Division in Nigeria, the poet's implication becomes clearer. The preaching of the Church is no better than the warnings of a mere madman – 'Jadum'.

The preaching becomes rather hypocritical in 'Initiation (iv)'. It says 'Screen your bedchamber thoughts / with sunglasses' so that there will be **18** no interference from outside with man's mind. This is encouraging hypocrisy. Provided you do something in hiding, there is nothing wrong in doing it – Victorian morality? But the poet proves the argument wrong, for the 'prophet' and the 'poet' can probe the mind's chamber.

Finally, in section (v) comes the command, to the poet impossible of obedience, demanding that the ram should 'disarm'. The poet responds:

> except by rooting
> who could pluck yam tubers
> from their base?

The reference here is to the life of celibacy which is imposed upon the Catholic priests. To forbid a young man from having sex is like asking a ram to disarm, and that is to say that it should not use its genital organ. The poet here observes that the only way in which one can stop a ram (or a young man) from having sex is to cut the sex organ from the ram or the man, and this is like digging up 'yam tubers' from the earth. The poet here means of course that the Church gives an impossible command. This interpretation generally agrees with that given by Paul Theroux.[8]

The sorrowful, almost pitiable, picture of the Convent Sisters in 'Silences' constitutes one more facet of Okigbo's satirical attack on the Catholic Church. The poem opens with the sisters showing self-pity, and moves through fear and complaint to resignation. They are 'dumb bells'; even though their worlds 'flourish' they are still 'our worlds that have failed', and their own song to them is 'our swan song'. The sisters do not marry or bear children; at least they are not supposed to do so. The poet here condemns this institution of the Catholic Church and does so effectively by making the sisters sing the futility of themselves and their life.

RELIGIOUS REVIVAL

Since Christopher Okigbo could not be accommodated any longer in the Catholic religion where he felt exiled, he decides to go back to the indigenous religion to revive it for himself and retain it. Thus in 'Idoto' (*Heavensgate*) the poet stands before 'mother Idoto' as 'a prodigal' desiring to return to her who is his parent and deity, and praying to her to 'give ear and hearken' to his 'cry'. Paul Theroux correctly observed that Okigbo is 'a poet, prophet, prodigal'.[9] He is a prodigal, an outcast, an exile (the word 'prodigal' is used three times in *Heavensgate*). And having had an unsatisfactory experience with the imported Catholic religion, he, like the prodigal son of the Bible, comes back home now to his parent, begging for readmission into the family fold.[10]

From now on, Okigbo's poems begin to teem with the apparatus of indigenous religious worship. He is now enthusiastic about this system of worship. He strikes the note clearly in 'Lustra (i)' (*Heavensgate* p. 30). **19**

The poet would climb the hills 'body and soul' for the purpose of 'cleansing' – purification; and for the sacrifice:

> Here is a new laid egg
> here a white hen at midterm

The scene of worship next shifts to the 'palm grove' in 'Lustra (ii)' (*Heavensgate*, p. 31). Here the worship will be done with 'Thundering drums and cannons/in palm grove', and 'the spirit is in ascent'. Also in *Limits* I, the poet worships the goddess of 'palm grove', who is the 'Queen of the damp half light'. He hands his egg-shells to her; he is an 'emigrant' leaving his religion of exile for her worship in the palm grove.

In 'Lustra (iii)' (*Heavensgate* p. 32) we get a mixture of Catholic and indigenous religious symbols. But while the Christian references are made satirically, the indigenous worship is carried out with genuine and serious intentions:

> Fingers of penitence
> bring
> to a palm grove
> vegetable offering
> with five
> fingers of chalk.

This time we have other items for sacrifice: 'vegetable offering' and 'fingers of chalk'. Like eggs, hens, and cocks, these are the things commonly offered to the gods of the indigenous Igbo religion. In the scene of sacrifice, it is also common to see drums being beaten and cannons fired. And of course the shrine house of the god or goddess is often likely to be in a thick grove. Furthermore, it can be noted that in the practice of the indigenous worship, Okigbo employs the tone of incantation, which is invariably used by every Igbo high-priest of the indigenous god.

O. R. Dathorne seems to have misunderstood this aspect of Okigbo's works. For Dathorne thinks that the destruction of the indigenous gods by the forces of Christianity implies the destruction of the poet's ambition to come home to his home religion and that therefore Okigbo only experienced a 'regeneration' within the Christian religion:

> . . . we get first a description of the ruin that is a *sine qua non* of the revolution of the spirit and out of this ruin comes about the regeneration of novelty.[11]

There is a revolution of the spirit in Okigbo, but he is not trying to revolutionize the Catholic Church with any view to making it better. This is not his aim; it is not even necessary for him. He has simply exposed this

Church with all the harm it has done to the indigenous values, which makes it unacceptable to Okigbo. The only choice left to him is 'homecoming'.

That 'homecoming' is uppermost in his mind can further be illustrated by reference to Distances; though this is a different kind of homecoming. In this poem, in which the refrain – 'I am the sole witness to my homecoming' – runs from the beginning to the end, the idea of homecoming assumes a tone of uncertainty, for it is to a dream that the poet is returning:

> . . . and the chamber descanted
> the birthday of earth, paddling me home through
> some dark labyrinth, from laughter to dream.
> (Section I)

Okigbo's period of exile in the Christian religion can as well be described as a period of 'dark labyrinth'; and he is returning to a dream which will quickly become a reality.

LITERARY STRUGGLE
Christopher Okigbo has struggled as much to establish his fame as a poet as to revive and preserve his indigenous religion. Like every artist he must have had to be cautious and wary, and must have had his difficult times with critics. His poetry is generally difficult and sometimes obscure. In fact it is sometimes so confused that it appears meaningless. When once he was asked what the sources of influences on his poetry were, he defiantly replied:

> My *Limits* . . . was influenced by everything and everybody. . . . It is surprising how many lines of the *Limits* I am not sure are mine and yet do not know whose lines they were originally. But does it matter?[12]

Okigbo seemed to be averse to commenting on his own poetry, as his reply above indicates. Thus in some of his poems he has dealt with the problem of an artist struggling for survival.

Limits II is about this theme. It is packed full with images of the desire for growth, struggling for light, and the desire for expression. We have a whole picture of a tender child in the midst of giants, or of an equatorial forest where the gigantic trees form a canopy with their leaves on top, preventing a low undergrowth from getting light and rain for effective growth. Very appropriately therefore the poem opens:

> . . . He was a shrub among the poplars
> Needing more roots
> More sap to grow to sunlight
> Thirsting for sunlight.

21

In the next stanza there are some 'selves' which extend their 'branches' into the 'soul', and they are in search of an audience which will listen to them. These 'selves' may represent different kinds of writers, for example, the poet, the novelist, the historian, the scientist, the philosopher, etc. The 'soul' may stand for the individual who is struggling for growth. In the end, however, one self triumphs, and the 'name' produces 'its foliage', which becomes 'a green cloud above the forest'.

The struggle to succeed as a poet in the face of other poets and critics and to attract publishers is quite a common literary experience. But in its usual extraordinary manner Okigbo's imagination has re-created the theme in such a way that one wonders if he meant to say anything beyond this. A reading of the poem however does not show that he has more to say than he has so obscurely said.

Limits III continues with the theme, but gives it a slightly different bent. The situation in which the artist is to create is very adverse. There are:

> Banks of reed.
> Mountains of broken bottles.

This setting, which is not commented on, is beautifully done. It is left to evoke all possible emotions in the reader; and one immediately gets the impression that to tread such places as are presented in the two short lines, caution is needed.

Then there comes the observation '*& the mortar is not yet dry* . . .'. This is said by way of reflection; it may be as a result of the realization of one's own immaturity, or the obvious impossibility, because of obstacles, of proceeding with the work. Tracing this line back to its source may help to elucidate matters. The line is taken from Ezra Pound. Pound's Canto VIII[13] deals with the Malatesta theme. Sigismondo Malatesta was an Italian Renaissance soldier, whose superb qualities as a schemer, strong man, and admirer of beautiful things, held much attraction for Pound. Pound learnt the history of this passionate hero during one of his tours of the Italian battle-fields, and in *The Cantos* (VIII, IX, X among others) he tipped him for commensurate glorification. Pound did not merely catalogue facts and events about Malatesta, but created 'letters and documents to give his "history" an air of disinterestedness'.[14] It is in one of those letters, which appears at the very beginning of Canto VIII, that the following instruction is given:

> And tell the *Maestro di pentore*
> That there can be no question of
> His painting the walls for the moment
> As the mortar is not yet dry
> And it would be merely work chucked away.

In the next eight lines we learn that the buildings to be painted are 'Chapels', and that in the interim 'something else' would be arranged for the painter to paint. It is the fourth line of the passage quoted above that Okigbo has adopted, and but for 'As' which is supplanted by '&' in Okigbo's *Limits*, the line is transferred intact.

In its original context, the line indicates an order or caution not to do something. It is prohibitive, even though not in a harsh way. In the same manner, in Okigbo the line advises caution, for the whole atmosphere is an unfavourable one. Landing on the difficult ground must be 'silent' and 'soft as cat's paw / sandalled in velvet' – words again showing caution.

The next stanza picks up the note of struggle which was dealt with in *Limits* II:

> So we must go,
> Wearing evemist against the shoulders,
> Trailing sun's dust saw dust of combat,
> With brand burning out at hand-end.

The phrase 'dust of combat' may have had its origin in W. R. Greg's *Literary and Social Judgments* (N. Trubner & Co., 2nd ed., 1869) in which is contained Greg's criticism of Charles Kingsley's *Westward Ho!* Commenting on the work, Greg said of Kingsley:

> ... the dust of the combat is to him the breath of life ...[15]

To Greg, Kingsley appears so interested in battles and bloodshed that it seems that the dust of the combat reflected in the book is the breath of Kingsley's life as a writer, of that particular work at least.

Kingsley is therefore not directly involved in the 'combat' that gave him inspiration as a writer. But Okigbo is involved in his own 'combat': he is combating the unfavourable *milieu* and all those people who, as we shall learn shortly in the poem under discussion, force him to sing tongue-tied:

> Then we must sing
> Tongue-tied without name or audience,
> Making harmony among the branches.

This is a height of inhibition, suppression, lack of encouragement, for the aspiring voice of the singer, the poet, or any artist. That is why Okigbo calls it the 'crisis point'. The voice shows some momentary success in the struggle; it is 'reborn' and 'transpires / Not thro' pores in the flesh / but the soul's back-bone'.[16] But this does not last long, for at the end of the poem (*Limits III*) we learn that:

>   . . . the dream wakes
>   and the voice fades
>   in the damp half light
>   like a shadow

and does not leave 'a mark'. If the whole struggle, however, is about having the poet's voice heard, as I think it is, it is more than a mere dream, and his voice has certainly left 'a mark'.

CONCLUSION

The generative impulse behind those poems of Okigbo discussed in this study is that which has resulted from conflict. It is the irresistible pressure of experience under which the poet was being crushed that has ultimately melted the frozen waters of his soul and released the stream of his songs.

William Empson has correctly observed that 'good poetry is usually written from a background of conflict'.[17] And according to T. S. Eliot, 'the essential advantage for a poet is not to have a beautiful world to deal with'.[18] Not only is Okigbo's world far from beautiful; it is a terribly ugly one which has been made more sordid by the negative and antagonistic forces of history. Since 'the negative is more importunate'[19] in the creative experience, these opposing forces have led Okigbo to a 'mature realization of the existence of both good and evil, an understanding that takes on a dramatic significance only when perceived as a struggle between these forces'.[20]

For Okigbo, the 'good' has triumphed in the sense, that is, that he has tenaciously held on to it to the end. The 'good' for him is traditional African culture with its religion, and the native African talent in him which has enabled him to revive and preserve that culture irrespective of the efforts of the foreign agencies to suppress it.

NOTES

1. Christopher Okigbo, *Heavensgate* (Mbari Publication, Ibadan, 1962).
2. *History of Nigeria*, Sir Alan Burns (Allen & Unwin, 1963), 264. This book was first published in 1929.
3. Christopher Okigbo, *Limits* (Mbari Publications, Ibadan), 1964.
4. *Black Orpheus*, No. 12 (1963), 47.
5. Sir James Frazer, *The Golden Bough*, IV, 221
6. Published in *Transition*, IV, 18 (1965), 16–17.
7. See *Transition*, V, 22 (1965), 18–20; and *Black Orpheus*, No. 15 (August 1964), 59.
8. See *Transition*, V, 22 (1965), 19.
9. *Transition*, V, 22 (1965), 20.
10. Luke 15.

11. See *Black Orpheus*, No. 15 (August 1964), 59.
12. 'Transition Conference Questionnaire', *Transition*, II, 5 (July–August 1962), 12.
13. *The Cantos of Ezra Pound* (London, 1964), p.32.
14. See William Van O'Conner, *Ezra Pound* (Minneapolis, 1963), pp. 35–6.
15. Quoted in Robert Bernard Martin's *The Dust of Combat: A Life of Charles Kingsley* (London, 1959), p. 178.
16. Cf. Matthew Arnold's words: '... genuine poetry is conceived and composed in the soul'. See Arnold's *Essays in Criticism* First and Second Series (London, 1964), p. 279.
17. William Empson, *Seven Types of Ambiguity* (New York, 1955), p. xv.
18. T. S. Eliot, *The Use of Poetry and the Use of Criticism* (London, 1948), p. 106.
19. T. S. Eliot, *The Sacred Wood: Essays on Poetry and Criticism* (New York, 1964), p. 169.
20. F. O. Mathiessen, *The Achievement of T. S. Eliot* (New York, 1959), p. 68.

Obscurity and Commitment in Modern African Poetry

Donatus I. Nwoga

The African intellectual *élite* – particularly the sensitive among them – are a rather serious group of people. The many problems that beset African political and social development explain why. Much of the criticism of African literature by Africans has demanded that the writers show the same sense of seriousness, a sense of responsibility towards finding solutions to the internal and external problems of Africa, a sense of commitment. Two recent statements of the case will serve as illustration. Adeola James, in an article[1] with a variety of misconceptions, makes one clear point:

> Our literature must be seen as part of the struggle for the liberation of Africa, politically and morally. It must reflect a full respect for the value of human life, our aspirations and that of humanity in general . . . Any creative writing by an African where the writer is motivated not by the desire to speak his mind about the African dilemma but by the desire to please a foreign audience, deserves not to be classified as African literature.

On the basis of this principle she declares that 'African Literature is far from achieving its goal'.

Professor Ali Mazrui, writing on a higher critical level,[2] made about the same demand on the poets in particular. His is not a call for large political themes, but a concern for meaningful communication in the traditional sense:

> The dilemma facing African poetry in English is whether or not it should bother to establish a connection with forms of poetic expression in Africa antedating the coming of the English language . . . The question that arises is whether, if Protestantism and liberalism in Africa have to be tamed and traditionalized, the canons of literary creativity in the English language should be similarly Africanized. Is poetry which is totally abstract as alien to Africa as is *laissez faire* liberalism or egotistical Protestantism? For me the answer to the second question is an emphatic 'Yes' . . .

Fidelity to the traditional norms, he suggests, would give rise to intelligibility and meaning. Implying that modern African poetry, especially that of Christopher Okigbo, is the opposite, he praises traditional Swahili poetry for its meaningful communication. 'There are themes to follow, tales to tell. There is a concreteness of the *whole*, rather than a mere solidity of parts.' He demands the same of the modern African poet.

> I claim that it is in (the) mediate area of versified intelligibility and meaning that the English language can be made to forge a connection with indigenous poetic traditions of folktales, conversation and meaningful recounting of personal moments of experience.

These are overstated cases, due, to some extent, to frustration with achieving an understanding of what the poet is trying to say. But the basic point has validity, and this paper explores to what extent the poets have reacted successfully to the challenge. To restate the case: the challenge is two-fold – that the poet, through his art, contributes to the total of national, nay human, cultural and therefore social and spiritual growth; and that his use of language should not be such that his contribution is unavailable to the community. I will also state, by the way, here that my attitude to the issue is that put succinctly by Balachandra Rajan in his talk to the Conference on Commonwealth Literature in Leeds in 1964.[3] Defining 'identity' as the 'process of creative self-realization' and 'nationality' as the 'establishing of a collective myth or image' he said:

> To create an identity is part of the essential business of an artist; to arrive at, or even to contribute towards a declaration of literary nationality, is not necessarily relevant to his concerns and may even infringe on the honesty of his concerns ... The contract between the writer and his work is an individual, not a social contract ... But he is also possessed of the hunger for significance ... and no act of definition can be enduringly valid for him unless it is also an act of communication, the re-establishing of his identity with others, the rendering of an individual vision without corruption, into a public language.

It is necessary for fruitful discussion to point out the limits of reference of modern African poetry. Modern poetry, written in the solitude of the poet's privacy and printed for private reading, is at the periphery of activities. Its function is important but we must not spurt venom as if it were the most essential element in national stability and development. It is not available to our masses, who are illiterate and moreover do not understand the languages in which it is written. This is a loss but not a disaster in the African situation. For our rural populations have their culture and literature which are vigorously involved in the creation and protection of **27** *mores.* The following approximate translation of an Igbo song which arose out of the relief situation during the Nigerian civil war will show the immediacy of their literary reaction:

> Do you see what we have seen recently
> Have you watched what has been confronting our eyes
> If you imitate priests you won't go to church
> There was some funeral food that came to us
> Father ... built and locked a fence around it
> Those who don't bring chickens don't eat it
> If you don't come in a car you won't taste it
> And so we send our pleadings to God
> God who owns us
> Let him take pity on us: Let the war come to a good end.

It is well known that quite a few vernacular songs are being composed all the time in the villages and even in the towns, dealing with varying degrees of seriousness or humour with the failures and successes of society and private or public individuals, and expressing in general terms the deepest beliefs of the society. This is a vigorous and surprisingly growing, not diminishing, tradition, at least in my society. I doubt whether the growing tradition of modern poetry will soon displace it.

There is perhaps more ground for expecting our modern poets to be immediately comprehensible to students, particularly at the higher level of secondary schools. These are literate in the modern languages in which the poetry is written. One may request the poets to write some poems for school children – but this cannot be an absolute demand. The need to address different levels of intelligence and perception has been recognized in the area of fiction and there has been produced a mass of novels for the young (much of it unfortunately unsatisfactory in language level and structural development); and one approaches Achebe's *Chike and the River* with different critical attitudes from *Arrow of God.* The basic responsibility for making the poetry available to younger readers lies with critics and teachers; it is their responsibility to offer explanations of technique, and annotations to difficult words and passages, to the younger readers.

The discussion that follows is therefore based on the communication between our modern poets and the perceptive members of the intellectual *élite.* I believe that it is at that level that there can be a just assessment of their achievement in facing the challenge of meaningful and responsible expression and communication.

THE PROBLEM OF OBSCURITY

It is quite easy to exaggerate the problem of obscurity in recent African

poetry, for, of course, in absolute quantity more simple poems are being written and published than those that can be referred to as obscure. A complaint of obscurity cannot be made after a reading of *Darkness and Light* (ed. Peggy Rutherford) published in 1958. Both Langston Hughes's anthology *Poems From Black Africa*[4] and John Reed & Clive Wake's, *A Book of African Verse*[5] contain a ratio of at least three easily accessible poems to one obscure one. I have seen the first three issues of *Zuka*, the East African journal of creative writing, and there is not a poem in them that makes excessive demands on the reader.

The bulk of recent African poetry is therefore not obscure. But this majority has not received much comment or been brought to the forefront for a variety of reasons. For one thing, Ulli Beier and Gerald Moore, who still retain their pre-eminence and stature in the projection of African literature, preferred to include specifically modern poems – with all the implications of modernity determining their choice – in their popular anthology *Modern Poetry From Africa*. This anthology was bound to influence patterns of thinking on modern African poetry because of the editor's clear definition of the determining factors of their choice of poets and the high standards which they demanded in the poems they reproduced.

Another factor influencing the greater attention paid to the more complex poems is the rather unexciting and unchallenging nature of most of the more accessible poems. Many of the poems in *Origin East Africa* and those that have appeared in *Zuka* come within this category. This might be the result of the late contact of the East African *élite* with the culture of the English language due to the nature of the colonial policy of occupation attempted there. And most of the poets are anyway still at the student level and have yet to develop a clear voice. David Rubadiri's and Jonathan Kariara's poems stand out, of course, in their simple grace and sophistication. Occasionally also, when reading the journal one has a sense of frustration at finding that an interesting voice has spoken only once. It would, for example, be interesting to watch the development of N. Waiyaki, of whom the only poem I have seen is 'Nostalgia' in *Zuka*, 2. But, generally, it appears necessary to conclude that simplicity is a factor of artistic incompetence. There is a simplicity of language which is a result not of artistic control but of failure of knowledge; a simplicity of perception resulting from an inability to reach out to any subtle connotations from a setting, event, or situation; a naivety of thought which sees none of the varied implications, the subtleties and deeper reflections, attaching to a projected notion. These might be 'versified intelligibilities' but they do not make exciting poetry. The general impression is that of failure to follow earnestly in the traditions of any serious poetry, a failure to manipulate the transition from the traditional song in which the oral situation, the accompaniment of melody and dance and rhythms, add to the total artistic effect, **29** to the tradition of written poetry in which the total effect has to be from the words on the page. The simple conception of poetry as versified thought becomes a handicap.

On the other hand, it is this simplistic approach of the East African poet that has produced the most significant and arresting of the recent long poems, Okot p'Bitek's *Song of Lawino*.[6] It is as simple in its language and as nostalgic in its internal reference to the passing of tradition as, for example, Joseph Waiguru's 'The Round Mud Hut'.[7] But it achieves high imaginative intensity and communicates at a level that immediately holds the emotions. As Gerald Moore says 'Okot p'Bitek lends fire, imagination and tragic passion to his traditionally-minded heroine . . . [who] uses the imagery of traditional Acoli funeral and dancing songs, rather as Achebe's elders use proverbs, to give her song depth within the culture and enable it to drink from the abundant springs of inherited experience'.[8]

'Within the culture' in the above quotation is relevant. It shows one reaction to the challenge of poetic statement of the current situation in a borrowed language. And I think it is significant that p'Bitek first wrote his poem in Acoli and then translated it himself into English. His debt to English was therefore restricted to language.

The challenge of poetic expression has operated at more levels than language for some other African poets. Stephen Spender draws distinctions in the 'Introduction' to his *The Struggle of the Modern* which are helpful for the present discussion. He identifies three categories of writers. First, there are the 'Moderns' or 'recognizers' who deliberately set out to invent a new literature as a result of their feeling that our age is in many respects unprecedented, and outside all the conventions of past literature and art'; then there are the 'contemporaries' or 'non-recognizers' who are at least 'partly aware of the claim that there is a modern situation. Yet they refuse to regard it as a problem special to art.' For them art should be enlisted in the general struggle for human development. At the other end are those 'who as it were "carry on" and simply ignore the problems involved in being, or refusing to be, modern. It is not that they have nothing to say about modern life but that they seem unconscious of the need which has so obsessed some of their colleagues, of making abrupt changes in form and idiom.'[9]

'Within the culture' is significant because it points out that the achievement of p'Bitek is partially a result of his stability within the culture of the African literary tradition that informs his work. But there are others who fit into the category of 'Modern' as defined in Spender's statement, who, by temperament and training, have passed from this confidence, this stability; who, therefore, face not only the challenge of language but have **30** to find also the 'form and idiom' for giving expression to the complexity of their predicament. And the search for this form and idiom in a foreign language presents an extra dimension of choice of traditions to the problem, for, as Gerald Moore pointed out at a Conference in Freetown in 1963 'This encounter [of the African poet with the English Language] presents problems which are not being faced by any European writer, and which haven't been faced by the European writer for a long time ... Since the emergence of the vernaculars in the middle ages, I don't think we have had any corresponding experience of making this fundamental choice.'[10]

I do not consider 'modernity' a concept carrying its own value judgement. But it does describe a condition which provokes interest and analysis because of the experimentation and exploration which it excites. And I believe the first condition for the patient analytical approach to modern African poetry is to acknowledge that the poets are struggling to give expression to an elusive vision in a situation which they, as well as the intellectual élite which I consider their chief audience, find quite confusing. The resolution of the mental and emotional conflicts, the finding of a clear personal voice, would be a correlated process of slow but continuous development towards a new tradition.

In the search for this new 'form and idiom' the modern African poet has two traditions in his background, the African poetic tradition and the poetic tradition of the language of his choice. And both of these traditions have problems which he must solve to achieve an individual style.

The African poetic tradition achieves its effects through the matrix of its presentation (recitation, song, to the accompaniment of its social context, music, dance), through the inherent qualities of the vernacular languages (pattern of tones, alliteration, etc.) as well as through its sources and modes of imagery. The first two elements are not available to the modern poet, though I do believe that it is possible to introduce a rhythm which though not directly related to the vernaculars, is however derived from them.[11] The imagery is much more easily transferable. The effect of the use of traditional imagery in Okot p'Bitek's *Song of Lawino* has been mentioned. It is this usage that also reinforces the tragedy in George Awoonor-William's *Songs of Sorrow*. This type of imagery has reverberations beyond the individual situation and poem, linking the subject and the reader with the connotations of its intrinsic meaning, its social force and its previous usages.

But even this imagery has its problems for the modern poet. To start with, as translations the images retain only their conceptual content, losing in the process of translation most of the connotative literary effects of the original. Moreover what might retain its vitality in the oral situation which creates originality and force through re-creation, which is what performance is, can **31** turn to cliché and barren imitation in the written form. Writing captures and records the single image and once used the image may not be used again without the poet's repeating himself or being accused of plagiarizing the image from another.

Even more serious a problem is the change in the social picture, ranging from the external physical context to the patterns of thought, values, and relationships, that inspired the original images. Some traditional images are private to a group and a time in the symbolism of their physical elements:

> My fences are broken
> My medicine bags are torn
> The hair on my loins is singed
> The upright post at the gate has fallen . . .
> *A Leopard Lives in a Muu Tree*[12]

> Alas! a snake has bitten me
> My right arm is broken,
> And the tree on which I lean is fallen . . .
> . . . the trees in the fence
> Have been eaten by termites . . .
> *Songs of Sorrow*

Soon it might become necessary to write sociological notes to explain such images. Also some of the images will cease to be understood properly or will at least appear to derive from an insensitive imagination, when there is a change in values and patterns of thought and relationships. Here are two lines taken at random from an Ibo praise poem:

> Lion that drags out and kills . . .
> Lion that kills without enmity . . .

A sensibility that rejects even the execution of convicted murderers is not likely to accept in a modern poem an image that arises out of a context of an acceptance of killing as an indication of bravery and social stature – even if the world is reverting to barbarism.

But the change in outlook goes beyond even this. For example, Professor Mazrui made, in the article already referred to, a relevant point about the difference between Swahili poetry and the modern: 'In the case of obscure passages in Swahili poetry there was indeed such a thing as *"the* right meaning" of a given passage, and the task of the sophisticated reader was to discover what it was. It was indeed possible for a reader to be *wrong*. But the obscurity of abstract verse in the English language is calculated to leave a good deal to the reader's imagination' and quoting a passage from a poem of Christopher Okigbo Mazrui asked 'Can there ever be a *"right* meaning" **32** to such a passage?' The question does indicate a distinction between the public poetry of the Swahili and the private poetry of Okigbo. The difference between the uses of imagery proceeds from the problem under discussion – the change in attitudes. There was a 'right meaning' to the Swahili passage, not only because the images were public property, but also because they came from a state of certainty, from a tradition of stable and generally accepted values within which variety of interpretation was not easily possible. There is not a similar social and intellectual context for the modern poets. The old certainties have been shaken, and new stability has to be sought through a process of complicated balancing. The search demands first an introspective self-discovery and therefore a new idiom of which the 'true meaning' can only be expected to emerge with the maturity of new certainty, a new tradition. The following poem, an extract from a yet unpublished cyclic complex of poems by Kalu Uka indicates the problem I refer to, and its result on the type of poetry written:

> ... The world reels in the fluid beauty of all:
> The poet's wordy traction, the painter's usurped rainbows,
> The sculptor's lone begetting: these shatter on a palette,
>
> The chips of time. Only words incarnate the rhythms.
> And when love snaps and blood cools still
> I hear the split rhythm of synthetic sap
> Incessant, repeal the agonies of self –
>
> The echoes through raving coils of flesh
> And words and colours and blocks silenced
> In the extreme breast, feed the filth of genius
> Into the humdrum beat of unperceiving man.
>
> So when love ceases this trinity holds forth
> An immortal correlate diamond in these three-
> Fold dimension. The fountain of passion wasted,
> And the quartzed way to heaven is man's delusion.

The poem is involved with the problem of creation, with the dimensions of the creative spirit in its quest for order in experience, with creation as a valid vision of order. The poet presents this quest, not through a statement of the quintessence of the vision – that would not be possible at the initial stage. It is a new perception to him, it has a variety of implications and some not quite clear suggestions of other implications. So he has to go through the tortuous process of exploration and suggestion. Traditional poetry would give him no effective model here – if he had caught a glittering, shimmering certainty he might have been able to state it in the affective modes of tradition. With his search, his tentativeness, he has to find his own idiom and phraseology to express himself, and it is not surprising that the language is tortured out of normal shape. **33**

If the tune changes, the dance has to change. Lyndon Harries has a clear assessment in 'The Credibility Gap in Swahili Literature'[13] of the diminution of sensibility and fervour which could arise from a too-rigid insistence on traditional modes in a changed situation.

The foreign tradition, the tradition that came with the language and new literary education, also presents problems for the modern African poet. Professor Eldred Jones referred to this at the Conference in Freetown. '. . . Not that I think that anyone can stipulate how African poetry should be written, but conscious of the fact that we are writing primarily, I hope, for an African audience, should African writers not be a little more choosy about the models they adopt in English writing?' Referring specifically to Okigbo's use of Ezra Pound who is 'recondite and inaccessible to most people' as a model he concluded 'Now, unless our audience is to be outside Africa, African poetry is not yet ready to use a person like Pound as a model with great profit.'[14]

Ezra Pound is of course only one of those foreign poets who have exerted a strong influence on the technical approach to artistic creation among our modern poets. Partly because most of these writers have gone through a university education in which the study of modern poetry was required, also because of the greater and more culturally-liberated contact with foreign literature among the intellectual *élite*, they have drawn inspiration from a variety of external sources ranging through the metaphysical poets of the past age, to several of the modern American, English and European poets. What these modern poets have in common appears to be a certain rather pervasive love of distant and exotic erudition, a conception of the WORD as image and meaning which has led to the disregard of the normal, logical, syntactical structure of communication, and a dissociation of the poetic sensibility from the physical social group which has resulted in the enigma of private symbolism. The total of these characteristics is a poetry which is difficult to the point of repulsing the ordinary perceptive reader of poetry for entertainment, but which, however, presents some shattering flashes of insight when the perception behind it comes through.

It would not be legitimate to object to the use of such models on the basis of cultural nationalism. This is what is wrong with the attitude expressed in the call for a taming and traditionalization of the imported canons of literary creativity. A tradition-bound approach would be retrogressive and would, moreover, only imprison the creative genius. What should be expected would be a progressive approach, an expansiveness, a growth of imagination, a rebirth of the creative instinct sparked off by contact with new elements. Genuine criticism would then object only to cases where there is a complete break with the poet's creative self, a break **34** which would give rise to pure dead imitation.

In addition to the normal problems arising from the use of a foreign language which has its own cultural connotations, our poets have had, in using foreign models, the added problem of growing out of the imitativeness which the reputation of such poets has forced on them. Such imitativeness gives rise to the failure of much of the early poetry of even the most renowned of our poets. J. P. Clark's gymnastics in 'Of Faith' and parts of 'Ivbie' are undigested Hopkins, to whom he acknowledges his debt in 'Variations on Hopkins . . .'[15] There is no doubt that parts of Okigbo's early poetry overdo the obscurity: the abstract language, private imagery, supersophisticated word ordering and sentence construction, lead to such a lack of communication that one feels some sympathy for those who quarrel with it. Prolixity is the result when the poem fails.[16] Okogbule Wonodi, writing in *Conch* on 'The Creative Process in Poetry',[17] acknowledges the deficiency in one of his early poems 'Prologue' which he wrote when he was at a stage when he was 'so obsessed with sound that often the sound becomes the only preoccupation of the poem . . . I am not sure that it meant anything more than that [exploitation of sonorous words] when I wrote it. Certainly it does not mean anything to me now but I still enjoy the sound and its loud music.'

The modern European poets to whom our modern poets apprenticed themselves were difficult to understand and therefore even more difficult to imitate because their technical complexity could more easily divert the reader and imitator from the essential character of their poetry and their underlying perception of life and art. In the context of the development of our modern poets it is however understandable that these modern European poets were used as models. What we have is a situation which is a reversal of what might be considered the natural process. Instead of having a base of indigenous tradition into which new elements are introduced, we see our poets starting from the outside tradition and then becoming aware of their own tradition – because they are first literate in a foreign language and their first formal study of poetry is of the foreign-language poetry.

But as Ezekiel Mphahlele has commented: 'Every writer in the world is faced with this problem, always imitating somebody, whether he likes it or not . . . It then becomes necessary to make a conscious effort to develop something original. And if he is a conscientious writer at all, he will eventually clear it out of his system, and arrive at his own way of saying things.'[18] And, as Professor Dunn rejoined to Mphahlele's comment 'It is preferable to have Eliot as a master than, as in the case of some poets we all know, to take Alfred, Lord Tennyson'.[19]

Out of the two traditions open to our modern poets for the evolution of the new 'form and idiom' for expressing themselves, we find therefore that **35** along with the borrowed language, the modern African poets have borrowed the techniques of, and approach to, poetic creation of the foreign tradition. European poetry of the first half of this century supplied the models for the most enterprising of the poets. The unfortunate consequences have been mentioned. But there have also been some happy results, particularly, in the poems of the poet's maturity, for example, in Okigbo's 'Path of Thunder',[20] and Soyinka's *Poems from Prison*.[21] The emphasis on word and image, the projection of meaning through the cumulation of poignant images rather than through a mental logic of exposition have affinities with traditional African modes of poetic creation which may explain our poet's ready recourse to these models. Moreover, the experimental approach of the European modern poets has released the African poet from adherence to the strict metres and forms of earlier poetry and encouraged an equally experimental approach which has led, as the sensibility of the poets developed and they acquired their own voices, to the perceptive introduction and stabilization of elements from traditional African poetry into their work. But it is to be expected that with the gaining of more stability in the new culture, the poets will tend to follow a tradition which will be derived from a mixture of the modern techniques which have become domesticated by African poets and the elements of traditional poetry which are being popularized through research and study.

Finally, I think it needs to be pointed out that there are degrees and variations of obscurity in modern African poetry. As we have seen, there is a large body of poetry which is direct and simple in the expression of idea or feeling. Other poems have the semblance of obscurity because of their complicated syntax, and the reader needs only to restore the words to their normal order or supply the missing links to come to a position to appreciate the poems. Some other poems are found difficult because they are involved in the exploration of ideas which, in the first place, are difficult of comprehension to many, or describing a situation with which the reader may be unfamiliar. In this case, glossaries and explanations will open the way to appreciation. In other poems the vastness of the poet's field of reference is the source of obscurity. The poet takes his images and figures from areas ranging from distant civilizations through a variety of literary sources to local myths, legends, and rituals, and it would require the same breadth of reference for the reader to come to grips with his work.[22]

Two sources of obscurity remain, and these offer more problems to the conscientious reader. The first arises from the tendency of the poet to give unusual and private symbolic meaning to his images. This is where the break with African tradition is most pronounced. And this is where the experimental nature of modern poetry can lead the unwary or unconscientious poet astray. I suggest however that the successful creative poet, through a continuous and sincere usage, finally clarifies the meaning of his symbols which then pass into the tradition.

The second of the causes of complexity is that which belongs as much to the 'modern' as to the traditional approach to poetic creation and presents a nearly insurmountable problem to a mind restricted to the logical mode of poetic creation. It operates on the level of continuity of symbolic meaning, using images which on their literal level either make no meaning or even appear to conflict. Passages are constructed with the metaphors as their semantic constituents. This approach produced for example Awoonor-Williams' *Songs of Sorrow* and Christopher Okigbo's *Path of Thunder*. It demands that the reader escape from the clutches of logical mental sequence and release the mind and imagination to reach out and acquire the impact of images which accumulate to drum in their meaning.

As Christopher Okigbo himself said, making a distinction between 'meaning' and 'significance' which is valid in his context but which I have found unnecessary in my discussion:

> Because what we call understanding – talking generally of the relationship between the poetry-reader and the poetry itself – passed through a process of analysis, if you like; there is an intellectual effort which one makes before one arrives at what one calls the meaning. Now, I think it possible to arrive at a response without passing through that process of intellectual analysis, and I think that if the poem can elicit a response in either physical or emotional terms from an audience, the poem has succeeded. I don't think that I have ever set out to communicate a meaning. 'It is enough that I try to communicate experiences which I consider significant.'[23]

Obscurity of itself is, of course, not a virtue. Rather it is an obstruction. And one recognizes that it could be spurious, a cloak for absence of meaning and feeling, a game played on the reader by a smart seeker of fame. What I have tried to do is to show that there are cases where the obscurity of a poem is only on the surface and to suggest that in cases of genuine obscurity resulting from creative inventiveness towards new expression, we might find the poems worthy of the labour of intensive study towards explication. Time, study, and critical commentary, will combine to reduce genuine obscurity and dismiss the polemics about presumed obscurity. Then it might be easier to judge fairly the achievement of the poets in facing the challenge of artistic expression in our modern situation.

THE QUESTION OF COMMITMENT

Much of the discussion on obscurity has of course arisen from a genuine demand that the poets should speak to us about matters of common concern. The failure to communicate would amount to a lack of commitment **37** whatever the themes the poets chose. I have tried to show above that there is a tendency to exaggerate this lack of communication. (I say exaggerate because it would be falsifying the case to assert that all the poems do communicate to me. It has not been possible up to this moment for me to make any beyond a vague, generalized, meaning out of Okigbo's *Distances*. And I have read critical commentaries and attempts at explication of that poem – Dathorne,[24] Sunday Anozie,[25] Moore,[26] and find that they stay on the level of vague generalizations, or fit elements – not the whole of the poem – into preconstructed moulds. But some poems which were impossible a few years back have yielded their meaning to insistent searching.)

In the discussion that follows one function of art is left out of consideration: art as a valid complement to action in the matter of commitment, which is being conceived as an effort towards making life more meaningful and satisfying to individuals within the community. Many who compare the African's attitude to art to that of Western man, tend to underrate the extent to which art A S A R T was held in high esteem in African tradition as contributory to communal well-being. In spite of its content of moral statement, the art of literature indeed held a lower place in the African community than that of drumming and dancing. A few writers now realize this.[27] The point here is that pure artistry with words must be recognized as contributing a dimension of satisfaction which cannot be lightly dismissed by recourse to either African or modern tradition.

It is necessary to review the implications of commitment as it relates to African poets. At the crudest level would be the demand, represented by the passage quoted at the beginning of this essay, calling for the poets to be 'part of the struggle for the liberation of Africa, politically and morally'. On the basis of this type of approach, it would be possible to dismiss most of the modern poets in contrast to the earlier poets. To the pioneers of our modern poetry, from the South African 'UHadi Waseluhlangeni', who wrote in the 1880s to the anonymous Sierra Leonean author of the Krio poem, 'For Dear Fatherland' in 1907,[28] to the better known R. G. Grail Armattoe and Michael Dei-Anang of Ghana, Osadebay of Nigeria, Gladys Casely-Hayford and Thomas Decker of Sierra Leone, the common theme of Africa overrode other concerns. Political poems – 'Africa', 'Africa Sings', 'Dear Africa', 'To the Woman of New Africa', and moral poems of the 'Let's Live in Peace' type, reproduce the conceptions of poetry under which the pioneers operated, a conception not far from mere 'versified intelligibilities'. This approach not only suited their minds but fitted in with the nature of the poets' activities. The poetry was part of their life – a public life committed to the struggle for the 'liberation of Africa, politically and morally'.

There can be no doubt that this was a valid form of commitment in **38** verse. And the failure of much of the poetry of that period to achieve artistic effectiveness was a result, not of the subject matter, but of the artistic incompetence and inexperience of the individual poets. The rejection of their work by the modern poets, along with the rejection of the concept of negritude by these same poets, led to an attitude which was validly criticized by Lewis Nkosi in 1962. 'The young writers of Nigeria can also be charged with a local form of romanticism; too often they regard their writing as a private human activity. The symbolism of their soliloquies becomes convoluted, private and obscure . . . This sharp separation between literature as an art form and its content has resulted in a kind of poetry and drama which seems to shy away from social criticism.'[29]

This comment pointed in the right direction. But it is also educative to inquire into the nature and causes of this introspection, and I believe that such an inquiry might lead us to other dimensions of commitment which could complement the more public and direct form exhibited by the pioneers and Negritude poets.

Differences exist between the lives and social contexts of the past and present. Where the pioneers were members of a new educated *élite* involved, by the circumstances of their prominence, in the political struggle for independence, the later poets belong to a more diffuse community of educated people with only a peripheral influence on the course of events. And the issues are less clear. The large public events of colonialism, setting up a dichotomy of indigenous ruled and foreign rulers, therefore calling for large and flamboyant public gestures, have given way to an internal situation of nagging minor issues. These issues are minor not in terms of their social consequences but because they break up into many facets that cannot easily be visualized in one big apocalyptic concept. Introspection becomes an understandable reaction in such a situation. It becomes both a means of self-defence from factors of social disorganization so pervading that a sensitive mind cannot cope with them, a symptom of the individualism that develops from alienation, and a positive factor in its instigation of a search for the meaning of life within such a context.

Commitment should be seen therefore in its dual possibilities of external call to action or internal orientation of awareness. A religion preached by unregenerate priests will hardly have consistency and will hardly succeed in converting many. In many ways, Africa's problems, which have provoked the call for commitment among our writers, have been complicated by the uncertainties of the moral, psychological, and social, bases for tackling them. Time spent by the poet in self-exploration, in the many minor emotions and perceptions that make up a man's outlook and basis of knowledge and life, must be considered a valid exercise in growth. Proper poetic expressions of these concerns cannot fail to have the effect of changing men's consciousness and making them aware of what previously they **39** had not even guessed. The concept of commitment must therefore be released from its enchainment to public themes and expanded to be conterminous with the concept of significance, with the search for, and expression of, human values in public and private consciousness and life. Commitment then becomes a factor of sensitivity of the poetic consciousness to the environment and life at all levels within the society of the poet.

Part of the problem of serious assessment has of course arisen from the fact that the works of young poets who have achieved maturity neither in technique nor in thought have been taken too seriously and have received too much critical attention. Much of the poetry written in English before 1962 was experimental, except for the work of Abioseh Nicol and Gabriel Okara and an occasional poem by Okigbo, Clark, Soyinka and Awoonor-Williams, and should now be used for a study of the development of those poets who have grown to maturity. Many more poets are writing in Africa today and getting published in journals like *Zuka*, *Black Orpheus* and *Journal of the New African Literature*, and in anthologies. But they must be seen in the perspective of their age and maturity in life and art and not discussed as if they were the instant successes and perfect illustrations of modern African poetry.

Moreover, on the more positive level of commitment through subject matter, fiction and drama have certainly featured more of the public themes in modern African literature in English. Except for his earliest poems, for example, up to 1966 Wole Soyinka wrote hardly a poem that could be considered directly committed, whereas his plays and his novel hit directly at the problems in Nigerian society. But, as suggested earlier, the private themes have their validity and significance in establishing the identity, spiritual and psychological, of the African and his human values.

The point at issue then is not the nature of the subject but the maturity in the treatment of the subject towards achieving significance. The point is not whether the poem was provoked by a personal event (Soyinka 'Death at Dawn'), an encounter with a Monet picture (J. P. Clark, 'Girl Bathing'), a reading of some foreign poems (Christopher Okigbo, 'Silences'), or an international society dance in New York (M. J. C. Echeruo, 'Song of the Kakadu'), instead of taking its subject from corruption in African societies or neo-colonialism. Validity derives from the poet's going beyond the mere presentation of the subject, beyond the mere conveying of the pleasure or excitement derived from the subject, to the conveying of a 'statement', a vision of life.

Lenrie Peters's constant theme of the need for the individual to struggle on and find his salvation, Kwesi Brew's exploration of 'the individual's
40 need to renew his conviction, to re-establish his certitude' will serve as

examples. Their concentration on the individual's predicament changes the emphasis but does not conflict with the African outlook – for even within the traditional context of the supremacy of social norms only the unsocial tendencies, destructive individualism, were frowned upon. What was required of the individual was to develop his talents within the framework of his society. The prevalence of praise poetry in Africa is indicative of the society's push of the individual towards self-fulfilment. The emphasis of the poets reflects the greater strains put on the individual by the present social context, their wish to encourage the building of a satisfactory and fulfilling individual life-style, the need to make meaning, to establish a guiding faith that will ride the storms of social deterioration or oppressive natural inevitability of corruption and death. Their specifically African commitment is in their circumstances – their historical, social, and spiritual, environment. That they are African men reacting to a set of African circumstances from a sensibility developed from an African upbringing, and the unconscious conception of art influenced by their exposure to traditional oral literature, should have an inferential significance to the African reader.

The same relevance could be traced through Okara's poems of personal frustration, Echeruo's and Soyinka's reflections on intellectual and physical conceptions and situations, Awoonor-Williams's explorations of the conflict of past and present, J. P. Clark's descriptions of events and situations, Christopher Okigbo's lyric self-exploration. Failure of meaningful communication in any given example of their work would be a factor not of the private theme but of a limitation in the perception and exposition of the theme deriving either from an immaturity of thought or from artistic incompetence.

The argument for the private theme, of course, only answers the type of question J. P. Clark reports as having been asked by a Russian lady as to how the author of 'Telephone Conversation' could write 'Requiem'. It in no way argues against the validity of the public theme. And it is observable that with the increase in political and social tensions there has been a corresponding increase in attention to public subjects.

One result of the uncertainties of the present has been the growth of a theme which might be considered public but which the poets have explored from a personal angle: the relationship of the past to the present. The past, its values and traditions, has impinged on modern African poetry in a variety of ways. It has supplied symbols, images, and techniques; but on the more public level, it has supplied themes. Attitudes to the past have varied from Soyinka's near-rejection, through J. P. Clark's deterministic view, to Awoonor-Williams's near-literal acceptance. Okot p'Bitek's *Song of Lawino* presents a purely traditional view of life, though leaving through **41** irony a possible counteraction to that view. (One does not put into serious consideration naïve exercises like Waiguru's 'The Round Mud Hut' which regrets the displacement of mud huts by oblong houses with zinc roofs, and pots and gourds by enamel crockery.) The values of the past are presented as capable of offering at least a guide to current judgement, and Awoonor-Williams's efforts at rediscovery project a belief that the sterility, sickness, and instability of the present are a result of divorce from the beliefs and values of the past, from an imitativeness of new ways which breaks our continuity with the past.[30]

With regard to the more immediate, present context, the tendency towards a public commitment among modern African poets first manifested itself in the mood of their poetry. As Gerald Moore remarks:

The last three or four years have seen a perceptible darkening of tone, notable in Nigerian writing, as the first promise of national independence evaporated in the fierce heat of regional hatred, political intimidation, arson and military violence. And this darkening of tone was to some extent prepared for in works which, though not tragic in overall intention, conveyed in their satiric detail the spirit of critical and creative impatience which was stirring in the young generation of artists.[31]

For example, some of the poems of Lenrie Peters, like 'Homecoming' and 'We Have Come Home', reflect a post-independence disillusionment and yearning for fulfilment of some of the bright dreams that heralded African independence.[32]

Going beyond mood is the specific exploration of public situations. The Nigerian civil war and its antecedents, for example, gave rise to Okigbo's *Path of Thunder*, to Soyinka's *Poems from Prison* and miscellaneous poems in *Idanre and other Poems*, to J. P. Clark's *Casualties*, and quite a few yet-to-be-published poems by M. J. Echeruo, Kalu Uka, and many student poets. The South African situation has, of course, had a persistent oppressive effect which has created the dominant themes of South African poets like Dennis Brutus and K. A. Nortje. These poems are reinforced in significance beyond, for example, the pioneer poets, by the internal force and techniques derived from the concept and practice of private poetry.

CONCLUSION

The volume of modern African poetry is increasing rapidly. By 1958, there were a few poems scattered in anthologies of African writing and journals like *Black Orpheus*. In 1962 there were just two or three volumes of poems by African writers in English. Soon anthologies devoted specifically to poetry increased. Now there are many published collections of individual poets and I am aware of a few more awaiting publications.

The areas from which the poetry has emerged have also widened and altered. South Africa's Dennis Brutus has written more, but it must be getting more difficult for new voices to emerge in the apartheid south. West Africa has continued to produce more poetry. The tragic death of Christopher Okigbo has silenced that lyrical voice, but the older writers continue to speak with more or less vigour and many new names appear in journals and anthologies. East Africa has indeed emerged into more prominence than in the past and one may hope that the many young writers being encouraged by *Zuka* will develop into mental and technical maturity.

It is to be expected that modern African poetry will tend to be less obscure. At least three factors may contribute to this. The gap in communication between poets and audience will diminish with our greater acquaintance with their poetry and an understanding of the patterns of the working of their imagination. Recently, publishers have been incorporating in the collections notes from the poets on their poetry, as, for example, in M. J. C. Echeruo's *Mortality* and J. P. Clark's *Casualties*. It is of course legitimate to require the poets to say all they have to say in their poems, but in the alternative their notes offer some help to an understanding of at least the objects that inspired the poems and the sources of the imagery. Annotations of the type in my *West African Verse* (Longmans, 1967) and O. R. Dathorne, *African Poetry for Schools and Colleges* (Macmillan, 1969), even if sometimes tentative, will help towards understanding. Secondly, with the greater study of African oral traditions, and the growth of a confidence in African culture, it is to be expected that modern African poets will resort more to a unified African source of imagery than in the past, when a search for universality led to recourse to a vast frame of reference. Finally, the existence of a large body of African literature which is being studied in schools and universities is leading to the stabilization of a tradition of African Poetry. New African poets cannot but be aware of, and react to, this incipient tradition. Whether this reaction is positive or negative, the result will be a poetry which does not take its inspiration from foreign models but which will derive from African poets who will be progressively more easily understood and appreciated. Even its forms of obscurity will be more easily accessible to analysis and explanation.

The nature of commitment in modern African poetry will also tend to increase the desire of the poets to communicate more directly. Sensitive, sincere, committed to creating a meaning in life, the poets are bound to have definable reactions to the predicament of their fellow Africans. One calls to mind the tragic death of Christopher Okigbo and the two-year imprisonment of Wole Soyinka during the recent Nigerian crisis, the exile of Dennis Brutus and K. A. Nortje, and various other unrecorded acts of **43** physical and emotional commitment in which others have involved themselves. It is not inevitable that poetry of this new commitment will be about public events or that it will speak with a public voice. What is certain is, that whatever the topics which will inspire modern African poetry they will be treated in a manner that will develop among Africans an awareness of themselves and their predicament which will contribute in a large measure to the achievement of African hopes.

NOTES

1. 'A Role for African Literature', *Insight* (Lagos, July 1969), pp. 6–9.
2. 'Abstract Verse and African Tradition', *Zuka* 1 (September 1967), pp. 47–9.
3. 'Identity and Nationality', *Commonwealth Literature*, ed. John Press, pp. 106–9.
4. *Poems from Black Africa*, ed. Langston Hughes, Indiana University Press, 1966.
5. *A Book of African Verse*, ed. J. Reed and C. Wake (Heinemann, London, 1964).
6. East African Publishing House (Nairobi, 1966).
7. *Origin East Africa*, ed. David Cook (Heinemann, London, 1965), pp. 4–5.
8. *The Chosen Tongue*, Gerald Moore (Longmans, London, 1969), p. 156.
9. *The Struggle of the Modern* (Methuen U.P., 1965), pp. x–xi.
10. 'The Language of Poetry', Ch. 11 of *African Literature and the Universities*, p. 96.
11. This was a subject of heated discussion at the Freetown Conference referred to above. Gerald Moore, over-reacting to Janheinz Jahn and his Rhumba Rhythm, insisted, 'English is not a tom-tom, and it only sounds boring when it is played like one. When an African poet has something to say, I think he will find a way of expressing it in English . . . We shall not get very far by demanding that he writes in "African rhythms", whatever that may mean,' though, on another occasion, he admitted 'a certain deliberate weight in the utterances in Mazisi Kunene's "To the Proud", a rhythmic quality derived from the vernacular tradition'. Professor Dunn, on the other hand, insisted on the presence of 'something, certainly in the languages, a rhythm which can be brought across' and he referred to the transmitting of this 'native rhythm, the native music' into the English language by Irish writers. George Awoonor-Williams was not quite sure. 'I have a feeling that it is normally a general impression of capturing a certain essence of these things (drums, indegenous music), but not getting them into English in pure form because that is entirely impossible.'
African Literature and the Universities, p. 86–7, 103, 113–14.
12. Jonathan Kariara, *Zuka* 1, p. 35.
13. *BASHIRU*, a Journal of the Department of African Languages and Literature (University of Wisconsin, spring, 1970), pp. 37–41.

14. *African Literature and the Universities*, pp. 82–3.
15. These early poems will be found in J. P. Clark, *Poems* Mbari (1963). Some of them are not reproduced in later collections.
16. Cf. J. P. Clark, 'The Communication Line Between Poet and Public', *African Forum*, 3: 1 (summer, 1967), pp. 42–53.
17. *Conch*, Vol. 1, No. 2 (September 1969), pp. 48–55.
18. *African Literature and the Universities*, p. 83.
19. *Ibid.*
20. *Black Orpheus*, 2: 1 (February 1968), pp. 5–11.
21. Rex Collings Ltd. (London, 1969).
22. J. P. Clark, *op. cit.*, p. 52.
23. *The Journal of Commonwealth Poetry*, 5 (1968), pp. 89–90. Quoted in O. R. Dathorne, 'Ritual and Ceremony in Okigbo's Poetry'.
24. O. R. Dathorne, *op. cit.* – brief comment on 'Distances' on p. 90.
25. Sunday Anozie, 'A Structural Approach to Okigbo's Distances', *Conch*, 1: 1 (1969), pp. 8–14.
26. Gerald Moore, *The Chosen Tongue* (Longmans, London, 1969) pp. 172–5, the nearest approach to a meaningful reading of the poem.
27. Cf. Ruth Finnegan, *Limba Stories and Story Telling* (Oxford, 1967), pp. 25–7.
28. *Sierra Leone Weekly News* (13 July 1907). Reprinted in Fyfe, ed., *Sierra Leone Inheritance*, pp. 308–12.
29. *Africa Report* (December 1962), p. 31.
30. Cf. Gerald Moore, *The Chosen Tongue*, Chapter 9.
31. *Ibid.*, p. 191.
32. Eldred Jones 'African Literature 1966–67', *African Forum*, 3: 1 (summer, 1967), p. 10.

East African Poetry

Timothy Wangusa

Up to 1966 poetry in English by East Africans was slight and scattered, and mostly to be found in student magazines. Then with the emergence of Okot p'Bitek's *Song of Lawino* a door seems to have been thrown open for a flood of poetry,[1] and currently poetry is a most popular genre. By the end of 1971 not fewer than six poets had each published at least one long poem or a book of poems.[2] There were altogether six long poems, all from Uganda, and five books of poems. In addition there were two poetry anthologies: *Drum Beat* (E.A.P.H., 1967) edited by Lennard Okola, and *Poems from East Africa* (Heinemann Educational Books, 1971) edited by David Cook and David Rubadiri. In Okola's anthology twenty-one poets were represented, in the Cook and Rubadiri anthology fifty, only six of whom had appeared in Okola's collection. Here figures are of importance, as not such a long while ago there was not very much to count.

Song of Lawino was not only the first long East African poem in English but was also acclaimed as a pioneer in a new art form. Though in the tradition of dirges and elegies, that is to say, on the common theme of expressing sorrow at some death or loss, the formal organization of the poem is in a class of its own. It runs into thirteen movements of what we may call an extended dramatic monologue uttered in public. The internal structure is that of a dialogue, or a debate: a debate between two sets of values, Western and African, symbolized in the persons of Lawino, on the one hand, and Ocol her husband, on the other. But it is something of a 'free' and not organic structure, as a reshuffling of certain of the middle sections of the poem could cause no conceivable disturbance: the 'naïve' Lawino seems to move from topic to topic as they arise in her mind, and she simply lists them.

In terms of diction and imagery *Song of Lawino* demonstrates that freedom-from-Europe which it advocates with regard to culture. For Okot there are no poetic and unpoetic words: all words are possible, and **46** Lawino's description of the inside of an urban latrine offers a possible instance of words that, according to an archaic idea of poetic diction, would be dismissed as too vulgar. Here too there are no studied or classical images; the images are prescribed by the village.

Okot's next poem, *Song of Ocol*, must be read as a sequel and a reply to *Song of Lawino*. It is a restatement and an elaboration in the first person of Ocol's point of view as we find it reported by Lawino in *Song of Lawino*. But Ocol does not offer a parallel or comparable argument. With an assumed superior posture he rules that the new, glorious Africa cannot be built on the misery, ignorance, blackness, and inferiority of the past. Africa's past must be destroyed.

Partly because he does not believe his own bombast, and partly because his author does not agree with him, Ocol does not rise to the stature of Lawino. His mock-heroic tone undercuts his very shaky convictions, and his learned references ring hollow. As R. C. Ntiru has pointed out in his review of the poem:

> Ocol's stature is less than that of Lawino with her fire of attack, vigour of challenge, conviction of assertion and freshness of genuine self-praise.[3]

The truth is that Ocol is passionless and, as such, sounds airy and unconvincing. Indeed he is at his most powerful when he is faithfully describing some aspect of traditional life – before he jettisons it:

> You proud Kalenjin . . .
> When your spears
> Appeared on the horizon
> Beyond the Bahr el Ghazal
> The Nilotes scattered
> Like flying debris
> From a bombed house . . .

In his latest work, *Two Songs*, which includes 'Song of Prisoner' and 'Song of Malaya' Okot has moved from portrayal of culture-conflict to social commentary and criticism. So that in terms of theme or themes at least, Okot is not quite playing the trick of merely imitating himself and turning out 'songs' that are not singable.[4] His poems still continue to be monologues, with all the other characters seen through the eyes of the main protagonist. Also, apart from the fact that any poem could be defended as 'never speech but always song', in Okot's poetry, and particularly in 'Song of Prisoner', there are the recurrent song elements of refrain and the repetition of a phrase with variation. For instance, in 'Song of Prisoner', over and over again the judge's voice is heard asking the Prisoner: **47**

> Do you plead
> Guilty
> **Or**
> Not guilty?

And every time the Prisoner answers:

> I plead –

not just guilt or innocence, but some other unexpected 'sin', and a different one every time. The effect is one of great irony and shock.

A writer who will probably acknowledge direct indebtedness to Okot p'Bitek is Joseph Buruga. His *The Abandoned Hut* is not only divided into thirteen chapters or movements, like *Song of Lawino*, but is also on the very theme of affirming African values (in this case Kakwa values) against the encroachment of Europe. As in Okot's poem there is a single voice, accusing, lamenting, protesting, The accuser is the traditionalist and the accused is the Westernized African – with one reversal, that it is the woman who has gone European and the man who has remained faithful to African ways. And except for the fact that the relationship between Madiye, the jilted boy, and Basia was a juvenile one while that between Lawino and Ocol is a married one, the very ground of the lament in both poems is the same, namely, love that has been sinned against.

The two sets of values are presented much more schematically than in *Song of Lawino*. Apart from the first and concluding chapters, in each of the other chapters an aspect of life or a mode of conduct in one culture is contrasted with its counterpart in the other, and this is followed through with almost monotonous meticulousness.

A device that East African poets will have to be more careful about, as illustrated in Buruga, is the use of vernacular words. Where an equivalent cannot be found in English, or where the local African word will be better, perhaps with the help of a glossary, this can be very effective. But there is the danger of using too many of them, and often without justification. Why, for instance, 'basinga' when 'small' will do? On the other hand 'Kpekpe' (p. 23) for 'epilepsy' is an example of successful retention of a Kakwa word, which is better for sheer auditory, onomatopoeic effect.

What distinguishes Okello Oculi from Okot and Buruga is not so much subject matter as design and intellectual range. Effectively Oculi is also depicting a conflict of Western and African values. His orphan is literal as well as metaphorical, the latter being the new African who is a product of the unholy wedlock between Europe and Africa. The orphan boy who is at this level but a version of Ocol is presented to us from ten view-points, **48** on top of his own, as each of the ten characters with whom he is involved comments on his life. This device has the advantage of offering a variety of tone and an impression of complexity of situation. Also the fact that the central image, the orphan, is capable of more than one interpretation means that other images in the poem may lend themselves to similar treatment. For instance, the Wild Cat, 'Ngunydeng', is not only Death but also Europe.

Among Oculi's shortcomings must be included his excessive use of abstractions, his lame constructions and his uneasy collocations. A creation like 'song-boasting' (p. 19) is a delightful success perhaps because we can attach some physical expression to the otherwise abstract 'boasting'; but an expression of double abstractions like 'earliness's helplessness' not only sounds ugly but is too misty for good poetry. His occasionally raw constructions will be illustrated by the difficulty met with in reading this fourth line of the poem:

> Cushion soothe fill of soft bellies.

Oculi will also use the most unexpected prepositions, which is perhaps not a sign of poetic licence but of innocence. And he will throw together words like 'tip' and 'hole' which do not quite consort together:

> Like the man of politics you carry
> Bad sayings about me
> At the tip of your bottom hole . . .

The two Ugandans – Taban lo Liyong and Richard Ntiru – who have recently published books of short poems have, in so doing, modified what was beginning to look a long-poem tradition being set in Uganda. Taban's earlier book, *Eating Chiefs*, is a retelling in verse of various myths of the Luo people, with the purpose, the author claims, of provoking other writers to treat their tribal literatures as raw material for further artistic creations. An assumption which is bound to be challenged by other writers and critics: Is oral literature to be looked upon merely as raw material and not accomplished work of imagination in itself? Taban refuses to reproduce the myths as 'received', occasionally interprets certain elements, digresses, and interpolates with his own imaginings.

His next book, *Frantz Fanon's Uneven Ribs*, does not, as one might expect, take off from *Eating Chiefs*. It is markedly different. The subject matter, the imagery and the references come from all over the place: classical and modern Europe, America, and Africa. In form and expression he is among the very 'freest' verse writers, defying all rules and guides. And yet a central preoccupation of his poetry is that of the very nature of poetry. In 'The Throbbing of a Pregnant Cloud' for instance, he says: **49**

Times have changed
Prose is poetry now
Perhaps thoughts are now poetry
And weather prattle
Prose

And from 'The Best Poets':

the best artisans are those:
with ears for sounds:
   assonance
      rhythm most
      rhyme least
      and
   consonance;
With eyes alert for the shape of poetry
its

```
                  A
          R       C       H
     I    T               E       C
          t               u
          r               e
```

Taban shares with Richard Ntiru a truly keen awareness of other literatures. Ntiru is a very society-conscious poet, and is always exploring and exposing something of the dichotomy that exists in the human situation, something of the shadow between the idea and the reality – in our attitudes and intentions and wishes and performance. (See 'Love and Images'.) On the whole he is much more in control of his material and expression in the shorter poem; in the longer poem he has a tendency to disappear into imprecision.

Ntiru's indebtedness to other literatures is a conscious one. There is undisguised borrowing from other poets: significantly from T. S. Eliot; but also from Blake, Claude McKay and others. Sometimes it is for the sake of parody, with very refreshing effect when it works, as in 'Ojukwu's Prayer' (cf. Claude McKay's 'If We Must Die'). In 'The Chorus of Public Men', which is modelled on T. S. Eliot's 'The Hollow Men', Ntiru presents us with dissatisfied, worn-out men who are much more concrete than Eliot's rather shadowy personages. The social setting is much more immediate, and for the East African reader the poem may easily have more appeal than its prototype.

If the Ugandans might appear to be establishing themselves predominantly with the long, bitter poem, the Kenyans seem to be settling for the short lyrical poem, and it will be interesting to watch the future development of the two forms in the respective countries.

John Mbiti is first and foremost a religious poet.[5] He is far from asserting a favourite set of cultural values, even in his one nostalgic poem, 'The Drums of Africa'. Of him it may be said that he demonstrates 'what it feels like to have faith'. There is hardly a poem of his that does not make some allusion to God, eternity, or death. God is always *there*, and the poet makes the point, as it were, of acknowledging Him in everything. A number of poems are direct re-creations from the Bible. And even in the otherwise secular poem about imperial evils ('The Aching Continent') God is invoked at the end to intervene as deliverer. In 'War after War', where he mockingly expresses man's yearning for yet another lovely world war, even the signal to begin, in the last line:

And the war trumpet is blown

distantly recalls the trumpet sound of the apocalypse.

Perhaps because Professor Mbiti is a pastor by vocation he seems to be at home with syntactical inversions, a possible influence of the hymnal, and with words which would be considered old-fashioned except in reverential language: 'babe', 'eventide', 'perchance', 'fount'. But it is to theology, no doubt, that his poetry owes the enrichment of the paradoxical and even the philosophical strain. He is indeed at some of his very best in the paradoxical poem, as when depicting the hardship of 'the poor Bedouin traveller':

Always struggling to live in a hard place
Struggling and toiling . . .
And always working in a fixed way . . .
But ever willing to live unwillingly.

Is this not poetry at its highest? Or take his 'After is Before', with its contrast of the topsy-turvy present, when:

How is why and where is not;
When is now and this is that;
There is here and here is there;
After is before
And wrong is right
And right is left.

and the sudden rectification as life is transhumanized:

And then
Wrong is not right
Wrong is not left
Only right is left
And wins at the end of time.

51

The simplicity is that of nursery rhyme, the tone at first childlike, then suddenly rising to a startling, terrifying proclamation. This is being tricked into the depths. And the design is apparent simplicity.

But Mbiti is not just a proclaimer of Christian values. In his poetry, as in his theology, he is always engaged in the task of finding English words for African experiences. In 'The Rainbow', which is perhaps his best poem, his coinage of the phrase 'the living-dead' to denote the dead in so far as they are still around, will serve to illustrate his ability to find words for non-English concepts and to circulate and popularize them.

Only one year separates the publication of Professor Mbiti's and Jared Angira's books of poems. Angira's greatest concern is not cultural, as with the Ugandans, or spiritual, as with Mbiti, but social. What the poet's travelling mind yearns for is a 'social ordering', and the statement of the poetry is that there is no such ordering. Instead there is prostitution, economic discrepancies, politicians' lies, and, incidentally, deculturalization. To be noted in this connection is the prominence of disorder and military vocabulary and imagery: life *is* a battle (p. 20), especially after social and economic systems have failed. Angira writes ironically:

> It may be peacetime we know
> but under the fig tree
> are clubs and shields . . .
> and all for nationbuilding (p.21).

Apart from the social aspect, another concern of his poetry is that of art itself: how to fashion a work of art out of the things one sees, how to reach beyond the 'unshapen clouds', for:

> . . . the beauty who combines
> All these once and always (p.56).

His less successful poems demonstrate that such accomplishment may well lie in the direction of simplicity. In Angira simplicity is definitely a strength. When he tries to be what may be called complex, he is in danger of saying the unphilosophical and the nonsensical. There is the occasional verbiage ('Calvary'), and the poems in which he does not see what he wants to say ('Masked', 'Trap'). His real power is to be found in the unpretentious poem, such as 'He Deceives', a beautiful riddle poem about the shadow, 'Contrast', 'The Song of the Ugly Woman', and 'In One Pot'.

Angira's poetry is full of energy and movement; it is full of violent action: ploughing, cascading, swimming, ferrying across, flying, rolling, beating against rocks. There seems to be the violent energy of creativity here, and Angira's next work may well reveal new experiments in form, as **52** a means to accommodating this energy.

NOTES

1. The anonymous writer of the editorial comment, *East Africa Journal* (July 1970), complains of the sudden invasion of East African Publishing House by poetry.
2. Okot p'Bitek, *Song of Lawino*, E.A.P.H. (Nairobi, 1966); *Song of Ocol*, E.A.P.H. (Nairobi, 1970); *Two Songs*, E.A.P.H. (Nairobi, 1971).
   Okello Oculi, *Orphan*, E.A.P.H. (Nairobi, 1968).
   Buruga, J., *The Abandoned Hut*, E.A.P.H. (Nairobi, 1969).
   Mbiti, J., *Poems of Nature and Faith*, E.A.P.H. (Nairobi, 1969).
   Angira, J., *Juices*, E.A.P.H. (Nairobi, 1970).
   Taban lo Liyong, *Eating Chiefs* (Heinemann, London, 1970); *Frantz Fanon's Uneven Ribs* (Heinemann, London, 1971).
   Ntiru, R., *Tensions*, E.A.P.H. (Nairobi, 1971).
3. R. Ntiru, in *Mawazo*, Vol. 2, No. 3 (June 1970) (Makerere, Kampala), p. 61.
4. Taban lo Liyong prefers to call them 'meditations'. See *Dhana*, Makerere Arts Festival Volume (1971), p. 59.
5. In the preface to the poems Mbiti modestly describes himself as 'more at home in Theology than in poetry'.

Senghor Re-evaluated

Julia Di Stefano Pappageorge

Léopold Sédar Senghor is relevant today not only because he is the present President of the Republic of Senegal and a leading political and intellectual figure in Africa and Europe, but also because of his position as one of the founders of, and leading spokesmen for, the negritude movement, a forerunner of the Black Power movement. Like the American Black Power movement, which is a revolt against the white establishment, negritude emerged as a reaction to the white colonial powers and their cultural values. The white colonial powers denied the existence of an indigenous African civilization: the negritude writers sought to prove otherwise by establishing, through an essentially intellectual movement. the historical and cultural identity of their people. Black Americans feel that the values of their group have been scoffed at by the white establishment, and they too are seeking to discover, and establish through the creation of a Black Consciousness, not only a cultural identity but a viable basis for political action.

Today black Americans, like the early negritude writers, are seeking their roots, their origins. They demand Black Studies programmes; they have an interest and a right to know all they can learn about African history and culture. But immediately they run into difficulty. Most of what has been written about Africa's history and culture has been written by non-Africans who were sometimes condescending, or not capable of understanding their subject because of preconceived notions. It is only within recent years that the African states have emerged as political entities, and that Africans have begun to write about themselves in the languages of Europe and the West, i.e. English and French. Much of Africa's best literature has been written in French, and not all has been translated faithfully, if it has been translated at all. The subject of this paper – the poetry and thought of Senghor – is a case in point.

54 When asked why he wrote in French, Senghor replied:

Because we [the Africans colonized by the French] are of a mixed culture, because even though our feelings are those of blacks, we express ourselves in French since it is a language universally understood, and since our message is addressed to the men of France as well as all other men. French is a language 'de gentillesse et d'honnêteté' . . . You will pardon me for saying it, but I know its [the French language's] resources . . . and it is the language of the gods. . . . The French is like a great organ which lends itself to every timbre, to every effect, from the sweetest lyricism to the thunderclaps of a tempest . . . Moreover, French has given us words for abstractions – so rare in our maternal tongues – where even tears can be made into precious stones. In our maternal tongues the words have overtones of blood and sinew; the French words radiate thousands of fires, like diamonds. They are the fireworks which light up our night.[1] (My translation.)

The harm which follows from a non-French-speaking student's reliance on clumsy translations of French-speaking African writers is not simply that he does not get the complete sense of the writer's meaning, but, what is worse, that he comes away from the work of literature with the feeling that the writer himself was awkward in his use of words, and maybe not of much literary worth after all. This is precisely the sense I had when I first read the poems of Léopold Sédar Senghor in *Modern Poetry from Africa* edited by Gerald Moore and Ulli Beier. Was Senghor a poor poet, or had he been poorly translated? An old Italian axiom equates the translator with the traitor: *traduttore – traditore*. By comparing a few poems of Senghor in the original French with the translations of Moore and Beier, and with those of Reed and Wake, I found that Moore and Beier had in many instances distorted the sound (rhythm) and the sense of the French lines. In French, the lines flow with sweet lyricism; in poor translations they plod with limping feet. To the degree that they were inadequate or clumsy in their translations, they were traitors to Senghor's artistic integrity.

In this article I will address myself to two closely-related problems: first, some of the weaknesses of the translations of Senghor's poems by Moore and Beier, and later, a discussion of what the term negritude means to Senghor.

The translators John Reed and Clive Wake* had the advantage over

* John Reed and Clive Wake's translations of Senghor are available in the following books:
Selected Poems by Léopold Sédar Senghor (O.U.P., London and Atheneum, New York, 1966).
Senghor: Prose and Poetry (O.U.P., London and New York).
Nocturnes: Love Poems (Heinemann, London, 1969, African Writers Series 71).
A Book of African Verse (Heinemann, London, 1964, African Writers Series 8).
French African Verse (Heinemann, London, 1972, African Writers Series 106).

Moore and Beier in that President Senghor assisted them in the translations of his poetry. They, in turn, have greatly assisted the English-speaking reader of Senghor's poems by providing faithful translations of his poems, and by including an informative introduction and an indispensable glossary to explain the African words they have retained in their translations. The glossary also serves as a guide to important elements of West African history and culture essential to a clear understanding of the poems.

Senghor, in his poems, seeks to explore the relationships between the black man and the white, between European values and those of old Africa, in order to show that reconciliation and unity are not only desirable, but indeed essential for peace and progress. He brings diverse elements together in his poetry not in a structural relationship, but rather in one that depends heavily on the element of rhythm for its unity.

In their introduction, Reed and Wake say this of his poetry:

Nothing can be defined by negatives ... poetry is a listing of things, a bringing of them together, in a relationship which is not structural or architectural, but rhythmic and living.[2]

'Nuit de Sine' is preceded in the Reed and Wake translations by a short poem 'All Day Long' in which the poet says that he is trying 'To forget Europe in the pastoral heart of Sine'. 'Nuit de Sine', then, is an attempt to evoke the mood of Africa: Africa, the woman who soothes his weary head after his long exile in France; Africa, who keeps alive the spirits of the Ancestors who guide and protect their children. Senghor divided 'Nuit de Sine' into four sections: the first is concerned with the image of Africa as woman and mother; the second with the drowsiness of the moon, the story-tellers and the chorus; the third with the coming of night; and the fourth with the mystery of communication with the Ancestors. Reed and Wake maintain these divisions, but Moore and Beier do not, causing Senghor's images and thoughts to appear unnecessarily jumbled. We can evaluate the translations by comparing them, section by section, with the original French.

Femme, pose sur mon front tes mains balsamiques, tes mains douces
  plus que fourrure,
Là-haut les palmes balancées qui bruissent dans la haute brise nocturne
À peine. Pas même la chanson de nourrice.
Qu'il nous berce, le silence rythmé.
Ecoutons son chant, écoutons battre notre sang sombre, écoutons
Battre le pouls profond de l'Afrique dans la brume des villages perdus.

Woman, lay on my forehead your perfumed hands softer than fur,
Above, the swaying palm trees rustle in the high night breeze
Hardly at all. No lullaby even;

The rhythmic silence cradles us.
Listen to its song, listen to our dark blood beat, listen
To the deep pulse of Africa beating in the mist of forgotten villages.
Reed and Wake

Women, rest on my brow your balsam hands, your hands gentler than fur
The tall palmtrees swinging in the nightwind
Hardly rustle. Not even cradlesongs,
The rhythmic silence rocks us.
Listen to its song, listen to the beating of our dark blood, listen
To the beating of the dark pulse of Africa in the mist of lost villages.
Moore and Beier

The first line is translated almost identically in both English versions, except that Reed and Wake chose to emphasize the 'perfume' element of *balsamique*, while Moore and Beier retained the original word. According to the first meaning in Webster's Third International Dictionary, balsam is 'an aromatic substance . . .'; the third meaning is 'something that heals or soothes'. Since Senghor intended to suggest both the elements of perfume and of soothing, Moore and Beier made a wise choice in retaining *balsam*. They were not, however, as faithful to Senghor's meaning in their translation of the second line. Note that the Moore and Beier line loses the swaying rhythm of the original, which is better retained in the Reed and Wake version. Also, 'hardly at all' is closer to 'à peine' than Moore and Beier's 'hardly rustle;' and *lullaby* is both more onomatopoetic and rhythmic than *cradlesongs*. Moore and Beier's choice of *rock* in the next line is unfortunate not only because *rock* connotes hardness, and carries a hard sound, but also because the single syllable shortens the line, causing it to lose the undulating, soothing rhythm of the original, the rhythm characteristic of a lullaby.

Moore and Beier's translation of the second section of the poem – the description of the moon declining, and the drowsiness of the story-tellers and the chorus – again loses the rhythm and some of the beauty of the original:

Voici que décline la lune lasse vers son lit de mer étale
Voici que s'assoupissent les éclats de rire, que les conteurs eux-mêmes
Dodelinent de la tête comme l'enfant sur le dos de sa mere
Voici que les pieds des danseurs s'alourdissent, que s'alourdit la langue
    des choeurs alternés.

See the tired moon comes down to her bed on the slack sea
The laughter grows weary, the story-tellers even
Are nodding their heads like a child on the back of its mother
The feet of the dancers grow heavy, and heavy the voice of the answering
    chorus.
Reed and Wake   **57**

Now the tired moon sinks towards its bed of slack water,
Now the peals of laughter even fall asleep, and the bards themselves
Dandle their heads like children on the backs of their mothers
Now the feet of the dancers grow heavy and heavy grows the tongue of
    the singers.

Moore and Beier

In the first line the word *mer* means sea. The word *sea* helps to create a sharper image than *water*, which in this context is too vague and indefinite. 'Dandle their heads like children on the backs of their mother': loses the metre – dactyllic pentameter – of the original.

Dodelinent de la tête comme l'enfant sur le dos de sa mere.

In French the line moves in regular, lulling rhythm, consonant with the image of a sleepy child nodding itself to sleep on its mother's back. Moreover, Moore and Beier's *dandle* is a less expressive word than *nodding*. Even worse, by changing Senghor's singular 'child on the back of its mother' to plural 'children' and 'mothers,' they blur the sharp, individual image the poet created in French.

    In section three, note the distortion created by Moore and Beier's *houses* for *cases* or *huts*, and more significant, *confidently* for the French *confidentiels*, which means confidentially or secretly. The word *confidentially* helps to evoke the quiet, mysterious mood in which it is possible for one to communicate with one's dead ancestors, which is the subject of the last section:

C'est l'heure d'étoiles et de la Nuit qui songe . . .
Les toits des cases luisent tendrement. Que disent-ils,
    si confidentiels, aux étoiles?

It is the hour of stars, of Night that dreams . . .
The roofs of the huts gleam tenderly. What do they
    say so secretly to the stars?

Reed and Wake

This is the hour of the stars and of the night that dreams . . .
The roofs of the houses gleam gently. What are they
    telling so confidently to the stars?

Moore and Beier

    The fourth section of 'Nuit de Sine' as translated by Moore and Beier has two major distortions. The sense of the first line, accurately given by Reed and Wake, is completely changed by Moore and Beier who do not convey Senghor's idea that the dead ancestors will communicate with their living descendants. Also, the image of a 'kuskus ball smoking out of the fire' called to my mind something like a cannonball. Instead, the *dang* of which Senghor speaks is a type of African food. Senghor suggests the image of Africa, the woman, the mother, warm with life and love; the mother who nourishes her children both in body and in spirit. Reed and Wake solve the problem of translating *dang* by simply retaining Senghor's word and explaining it in their glossary. *Dang* is a Wolof word for *couscous*, which is an Arab dish of flour steamed over broth.

> Femme, allume la lampe au beurre clair, que causent autour les Ancêtres
>   comme les parents, les enfants au lit.
> Écoutons la voix des Anciens d'Elissa. Comme nous exilés
> Ils n'ont pas voulu mourir, que se perdît par les sables leur torrent
>   seminal.
> Que j'écoute, dans la case enfumée que visite un reflet d'âmes propices
> Ma tête sur ton sein chaud comme un dang au sortir du feu et fumant
> Que je respire l'odeur de nos Morts, que je recueille et redise leur voix
>   vivante, que j'apprenne à
> Vivre avant de descendre, au-delà du plongeur, dans les hautes pro-
>   fondeurs du sommeil.

> Woman, light the clear oil lamp, where the ancestors gathered around
>   may talk as parents talk when the children are put to bed.
>   Reed and Wake

> Woman, light the lamp of clear oil, and let the children in bed talk
>   about their ancestors, like their parents.
>   Moore and Beier

Africa nourishes her children spiritually by sustaining the spirits of the Ancestors, and by providing her people with a sense of the unity and the continuity of life, and by maintaining the concept that the living, the dead, and the yet unborn, of the tribe are all part of the community.

'Paris in the Snow' is noteworthy as an example of Senghor's earlier negritude view, in which there was still room for hatred of the white man and his false diplomacy which barters in black flesh. In this poem Senghor, a devout Roman Catholic, identifies with Christ, who, like the African, was whipped, slapped, and humiliated, by white hands. (Tchicaya U Tam'si later took up the same theme in 'The Scorner.') He expresses hatred, too, for the white hands that exploited Africa:

> Elles abattirent la fôret noire pour en faire des traverses de chemin de fer
> Elles abattirent les fôrets d'Afrique pour sauver la Civilization, parce
>   qu'on manquait de matière première humaine.

> They felled the virgin forest to turn into railway sleepers.
> They felled Africa's forest in order to save civilization that was lacking
>   in men.
>   Moore and Beier   **59**

The 'forêt noire', was not only black or 'dark' as Reed and Wake translate it, but also pure and virginal, until the white man from Western Civilization came to plunder it because he viewed the natural world not as a manifestation of God's immanence, but merely in terms of material goods to be taken out of the earth and sold for cash profit. This is one of the elements suggested by the phrase

> pour sauver la / Civilization, parce qu'on manquait de matière première humaine.

Western Civilization is not 'lacking in men' (or experiencing a 'shortage of human raw-material' as Reed and Wake translate it) in a quantitative sense, but rather in a *qualitative* sense. It is not that the West did not have enough men for its labour force, but rather that Western man was lacking in an essential aspect of his humanity (*la matière première humaine* – the primary human material), i.e. the ability to apprehend in the natural world an integral order in which God is really present.

'Prayer to Masks' introduces a theme – the need for the black man to 'teach rhythm to a world that has died of machines and cannons' – which is similar to that of a later poem, 'New York'. One line of 'Prayer to Masks' is particularly clumsy in the Moore and Beier translation:

> For who else should ejaculate the cry of joy, that arouses the dead and the wise in a new dawn?

In French the line reads:

> Qui pousserait le cri de joie pour réveiller morts et orphelins à l'aurore?

I would translate it thus:

> For who can shout the cry of joy to wake the orphaned and the dead at the break of dawn?

The dawn to which he refers is the new period in history in which Western man, whose mind and heart was numbed by the mechanization of its culture, will become reawakened to a consciousness of his own emotions, of his relation to his fellow man and the natural and supernatural forces of the universe.

The poem 'New York' expresses Senghor's belief that the artificiality, anaemia, and sterility of white, Western civilization can be cured only by letting healthy black blood flow into its blood. Arnold von S. Bradshaw was **60** quite faithful to Senghor's meaning in his translation of 'New York', and

Moore and Beier did well to include his translation in their anthology *Modern Poetry from Africa*.

An improved translation of stanza III could be made by retaining the best elements of the two English translations under discussion here. The Bradshaw transla꞉ ꞉ is given below:

New York! je dis New York, laisse affluer le sang noir dans ton sang
Qu'il dérouille tes articulations d'acier, comme une huile de vie
Qu'il donne à tes ponts la courbe des croupes et la souplesse des lianes.
Voici revenir les temps très anciens, à l'unité retrouvée la reconciliation
    du Lion du Taureau et de l'Arbre
L'idée liée à l'acte l'oreille au coeur le signe au sens.

New York! I say to you: New York let black blood flow into your blood
That it may rub the rust from your steel joints, like an oil of life,
That it may give to your bridges the bend of buttocks and the suppleness
    of creepers.
Now return the most ancient times, the unity recovered, the reconcilia-
    tion of the Lion the Bull and the Tree
Thought linked to act, ear to heart, sign to sense.

Arnold von S. Bradshaw

In the second line Bradshaw's 'rub the rust from your steel joints' is more colloquial and in this case better than Reed and Wake's 'cleaning the rust from your steel articulations'. However, Bradshaw's choice of *creepers* for *lianes* in the next line is a disputable one, since in American usage of English one does not usually think of creepers as tropical creeping plants. In fact, in Webster's Third International Dictionary, the first meaning refers to crawling insects and reptiles, the second to 'servile opportunists', and, finally, the third to the tropical plant. Reed and Wake wisely retained the word *liana*, which can be found in a comprehensive English dictionary, and which does not call to mind the irrelevancies, in terms of this poem, which *creepers* carries to the American reader.

In the next two lines Senghor speaks of a rediscovery of the unity of life and the reconciliation of the divergent forces of nature, and of diverse civilizations as well. Senghor's essential concept here is reconciliation and unity: you will note that in his line about thought linked to act, ear to heart, sign to sense, there are no commas to break the unity. By using commas in his translation of this line, Bradshaw may have made it easier to read, but he violated the poet's intention. Reed and Wake do not break the unity and flowing together of images by the use of commas.

We would do well to note that the kinds of values Senghor stresses in his early poems – 'Nuit de Sine', 'Snow Upon Paris', and 'Prayer to Masks' of *Chants D'Ombre* (1945), and 'New York' from *Éthiopiques* (1956) are somewhat different from poems like 'Be Not Amazed' and 'Elegy of the **61**

Waters' from his latest volume, *Nocturnes*, published in 1961. The early poems praise the values and the cohesion of African life; they speak out against the sterility and hard-heartedness of white Western civilization, and proclaim the need for the sense of primordial rhythms in modern society. Senghor feels that the black man can teach the white man this rhythm. But although it is true that Africa has taught dances and rhythm to America and Europe, it is unlikely that Western man can derive the same meaning from these rhythms because of the limitations of his cultural heritage, namely the distinct separation which exists in his world view between the sacred and the profane. For the African, the dance:

> cannot be separated from the religious, for both embody the life force or vital energy which is the supreme value of life, and the separation of sacred and profane cannot be made as it is in Europe.[3]

Senghor's most recent poems deal with more personal themes – with the problems of the nature of poetry, with his own poetic inspiration derived from memories of his childhood and the landscape of his homeland, and with his prayers that he may return to the joy and peace he experienced in childhood.

'Be Not Amazed', is beautifully translated by Moore and Beier, except that 'the furious cannonade of the god', which is 'de Dieu' in French, should read 'of God'. This poem is less lyrical than most of Senghor's poems, and purposefully so: the poet is afraid that time is running out for mankind, and the frenzy of his music mounts as he changes from lyrical musical instruments to war drums.

'Elegy of the Waters' is an apocalyptic vision of the destruction of most of mankind by fire, and a symbolic cleansing of the earth by a rain which the poet has called down from God by simply pronouncing the phrase, 'Let It Rain'. In African thought the *word* is of a mysterious, miraculous power. The word can be creative or destructive. Thus one does not speak aloud of the possibility of evils to come, lest by pronouncing the words one actually causes disaster to fall. In the poem Senghor writes:

> Lord, you have made me the Master of language
> Me, son of a trader, puny and grey at birth. . . .
> You, in the unfairness of your justice have given me the power of speech.
> > Reed and Wake

In an interview with the French literary critic Armand Guibert, Senghor had this to say about his attitude towards language:

> 'In the beginning was the Word.' I said *Word* and not *Speech*. In effect, the 'word' was not the 'spoken word', but the word sung and chanted to

rhythm ... In the beginning, then, the word was locked within the bosom of God, who, one day, feeling lonely, and having no one to speak to, felt the need to create: to speak.[4]

(My translation.)

Senghor fully appreciates the creative power of the Word.

To understand better Senghor's sense that time is running out for mankind, and that cataclysmic changes must take place if man is to survive on this planet, we would do well to study the writings of Teilhard de Chardin, who had a profound influence on his poetry and philosophy. According to one book about the relevance of Teilhard today:

> ... the sole purpose of Father Teilhard's writings was to show man that he, unavoidably, is converging with other men in the dimension of thought. For a long, long time in man's history the convergence was not noticed because the growth of various social institutions had a divergent appearance as man spread over the globe. Nevertheless it was inevitable that the social institutions of which he is a part would ... turn inwards upon themselves and upon one another producing a convergent effect ... 'There is nothing ... that can arrest the progress of social man towards ever greater interdependence and cohesion.'[5]

The frenzy of 'Be Not Amazed' can, I think, be better understood in terms of Teilhard's concept that there is no guarantee of man's future on this planet.

Senghor's vision in *Elegy of the Waters* of the destruction which God will send to our planet before He will 'let death be reborn as Life' seems to have been inspired by Teilhard's statement that the tensions and anxieties we are experiencing in the world today are the characteristics not of 'a break-up, but of a birth. Let us not be frightened, therefore of what at first sight might look like a final and universal discord. What we are suffering is only the price, the annunciation, the preliminary phase of our unanimity.'[6]

It is impossible to give a brief summary that adequately explains all the scientific facts and cogent reasoning which Teilhard de Chardin presents to make his theory convincing. It is sufficient for our purpose – a better understanding of Senghor's poetry – to read Senghor's book of essays entitled *Pierre Teilhard de Chardin et La Politique Africaine* to understand the dynamic effect the philosopher had on the poet's thought and work.

Like Jean-Paul Sartre, Moore and Beier believe that negritude is essentially 'the voice of a particular historical movement, when the black race has given tongue to its revolt against white rule'.[7] They note that in recent years 'there have been signs that the wellspring of negritude is running dry' and that since the 1940s and 1950s Aimé Césaire and Senghor have been 'notably unproductive'.[8] However, as Senghor has said in his essay, negritude is no longer moving in the direction in which it began. **63**

Senghor explains his concept of the negritude movement in the essays in *Pierre Teilhard de Chardin et La Politique Africaine*. The book was prepared for a conference of 'L'Association des Amis de Pierre Teilhard de Chardin' which convened at Vézelay 6–14 September 1961. In the first section of his book, 'Négritude et Marxisme' Senghor explains that the negritude movement came into being as a reaction against the attitudes and practices of the colonial powers which maintained that the black mind was actually a 'tabula rasa', and for the colonial powers the blacks represented 'a race, almost an entire continent of human beings who for 30,000 years had not made any creative effort in the realms of thought, writing, painting or sculpture, music or dance. The African was a nonentity at the bottom of an abyss, who could only beg and receive: a malleable wax in the hands of a White God with pink fingers and sky-blue eyes.'[9] (My translation.)

The French colonial powers, maintaining that the Africans had no culture of their own, and that French culture was superior to all others, followed a policy of cultural assimilation. They even bestowed French citizenship upon the inhabitants of their colonies. It followed that the young intellectual Africans were repelled by European values and sought to re-establish their pride in being black through negritude, which Senghor defined as 'l'ensemble des valeurs de civilisation du monde noir'.[10] With Aimé Césaire he proclaimed that they were the first men on earth, and that the early civilizations on the Nile and Euphrates were created by black men who were later the innocent victims of white barbarians. Senghor, writing in the 1960s admits that this black pride of the negritude writers of the 1940s soon turned itself into racism. He agrees with Jean Paul Sartre's description of early manifestations of negritude as '*Racisme antiraciste*' – for, in fact, the early founders of negritude rejected all that White Europe represented – 'her reason, her art and her women.'[11] However, the triumph of Nazism and the disaster of the Second World War showed the negritude leaders that the fruits of racism were hatred and violence; that unless the climate of world opinion changed, the powers of Science would be put to the service of Death and world destruction. Moreover, they realized the falsity of the myth of pure races: the earliest races intermingled, and the great civilizations of the Nile, Euphrates, and Indus, owed their greatness to racially mixed peoples.[12]

Senghor then explains the attraction that Marxist philosophy held for early negritudists as being based on Marx's understanding of the working classes (the exploited African) at the hands of imperialists and capitalists (the colonial powers). But he goes on to say that although Marx understood man as an economic entity, and man's role in historical time, he is limited in his thinking by his very adherence to materialism and determinism and by his concern with only a small segment of the world population – the working classes of Western Europe. He had little to say of the role of the African in the dialectics of history. Also, Marx, limited by his materialist conception of history, does not address himself to the question of man in relation to Art, or to Religion.[13]

To correct the inadequacies and ambiguities of Marx, Senghor directs us to Teilhard de Chardin, who does not reject Marx's method of dialectical materialism, but rather improves upon it, showing that *evolution* is the expression of the dialectic of history. He extends man (whereas Marx confined him to an economic entity) to the realms of Science and Nature, Biology, Geology, Chemistry and Physics, which describe man as what he is – 'a cosmic phenomenon'.[14] Unlike Marx, who isolated man in the sense that he regarded him simply as *homo oeconomicus*, Teilhard de Chardin considers man in his many aspects – anthropological, historical, artistic, cultural and spiritual. Teilhard speaks not only of *Homo faber*, but more importantly, of *Homo sapiens*.[15]

Senghor's attitude towards the function of the different races is surprisingly similar to Teilhard de Chardin's, who writes in *The Vision of the Past*:

> . . . humanity, taken in its concrete nature, is really composed of different branches. Races exist, but that is no proper reason for the existence of antagonism and a racial problem. In order to escape this problem and save 'human dignity' as a whole, some people feel obliged to deny the manifest differences that separate the ethnical units of the earth . . . A mechanic is not an athlete, or a painter, or a financier; and it is thanks to these diversities that the national organism functions. Similarly a Chinese is not a Frenchman, nor is a Frenchman a Kaffir or a Japanese. And this is most fortunate for the total richness and future of man. These inequalities . . . observed . . . from the point of view of *their essential complementarity* . . . become acceptable, honourable and even welcome.[16]

Whereas Marx condemns us to a blind determinism, Teilhard shows how man can direct his own future. Accordingly, the Teilhardian view of Socialism would be '*la méthode qui met la recherche et les techniques – politiques, économiques, sociales, culturelles – au service de la Socialisation panhumaine : de la Civilisation de l'Universel. C'est l'Humanisme des Temps contemporains*'.[17] (The italics are Senghor's.) Senghor then explains that negritude has changed from a negative movement to a positive one. It is still based on the system of values of the black world, but now it is no longer founded solely on race, but on Geography and History, and is dedicated to the convergent socialization of all cultures in which lies our hope for the advancement and future of humanity. Quoting from Teilhard, **65**

Senghor says we must 'stop living on the surface of our being . . . because of an inferiority complex . . . and reawaken the world of energy now lying dormant in the abyss of our consciousness. We must count our values, and cultivate them'.[18]

Some Africans feel that Senghor is content to have the black man assume an inferior role in history: the role of feeling, of responding emotionally, rather than intellectually or even politically. As a poet he has emphasized the emotional aspects of the African experience, rather than the intellectual ones. The ideal he espouses is a world of individuals and societies in which the forces of reason and emotion work in harmony. But because of the manner in which he extols European values – especially those of France – he tends to weaken the position he takes in support of African values, by a simple process of overemphasizing the greatness of all things French. He is too much a Francophile (note his remark quoted earlier about French being the language of the gods) even for my American tastes, but perhaps he is not very different from other Frenchmen – especially his fellow members of the French Academy – in this respect. Also he tends to minimize the importance of the separation of the sacred and the profane which exists in modern Western man's world view. Once having experienced this break, it is impossible to see the world as an integral whole, and to perceive the rhythm of the vital life force as traditional man does.

Although I question Senghor's Francophilism and his somewhat naïve belief that African civilization can teach Western civilization to respond to primordial rhythms, I agree with him that humanity's hope for survival and progress lies in its efforts towards ultra-hominization. This I view as a deliberate effort on the part of men of good will all over the world to rise to a higher level of consciousness of their own humanity. The motto of Senghor's essay is 'Everything that rises must converge'. Before we can achieve the 'Convergence panhumaine' of which Teilhard and Senghor speak, we must be able to communicate with each other without misunderstanding. To this end it is of the utmost importance that translators exert their best talents and efforts towards faithful translations. They have the responsibility of maintaining the artistic integrity of the poets they translate, and if they fail to do this they do indeed become 'traitors'.

NOTES

1. Armand Guibert, *Léopold Sédar Senghor, L'Homme et L'Oeuvre*, Présence Africaine (Paris, 1962), p. 133.
2. John Reed and Clive Wake, *Selected Poems by Léopold Sédar Senghor* (Oxford University Press and Atheneum, New York, 1966), p. xvii.

3. Geoffrey Parrinder, *Religion in Africa* (Praeger Publishers, New York, 1969), p. 21.
4. Guibert, *Religion in Africa*, p. 152.
5. R. Wayne Kraft, *The Relevance of Teilhard*, Fides Publishers, Inc. (Notre Dame, Indiana, 1968), pp. 86–7.
6. Pierre Teilhard de Chardin, *The Vision of the Past*, trans. by J. M. Cohen (Harper & Row, New York, 1966), p. 233.
7. Gerald Moore and Ulli Beier, ed., *Modern Poetry from Africa* (Penguin Books, London, 1966), p. 25.
8. *Ibid.*
9. Léopold Sédar Senghor, *Pierre Teilhard de Chardin et La Politique Africaine*, Editions du Seuil (Paris, 1962), p. 17.
10. *Ibid.*, p. 20.
11. *Ibid.*, p. 21.
12. *Ibid.*
13. *Ibid.*, pp. 22–8.
14. *Ibid.*, p. 34.
15. *Ibid.*
16. Teilhard, *The Vision of the Past*, p. 212.
17. Senghor, *Pierre Teilhard de Chardin et la Politique Africaine*, p. 50.
18. *Ibid.*, p. 63.

Algerian Poetry of French Expression

Mildred P. Mortimer

Nurtured by the *fait colonial*, the French presence in Algeria, Algerian literature of French expression, with its roots in a legacy of conquest, came to the fore in a period of bloodshed. The French conquest of Algeria in 1830 was the last of a series for this North African land: Roman, Vandal, Arab, Turkish. Yet only the Arab invasions of the seventh and eleventh centuries and the later French conquest left their mark upon the indigenous Berber culture. The former introduced the Arabic language as well as the religion of Islam; the latter brought the trappings of the modern Western world and applied the yoke of colonial rule.

From the time of the Algerian defeat in 1830 until liberation in 1962, poets emerged to express the suffering of a colonized people, give voice to the pre-colonial past, and evoke hope in the future – in the promise of a new, post-colonial era.

The Algerian poet belongs to a rich oral tradition of poetry and song. In pre-Islamic society he was thought to have been inspired by the genies and was respected as a man of superior knowledge. Moreover, he served an important social function: he was a defender of tribal honour, a herald of important events, and also the voice of the commonplace, of the routine activities of ordinary people.

For a description of the role of the poet, we may turn to the Algerian poet, critic, essayist, Jean Amrouche, one of the first Algerian writers of French expression. As early as the 1930s, he began to record the oral tradition of his people, the Berber-speaking population of Kabylia:

> The poet has the gift of *asefrou*, that is, to render clear and intelligible what is not . . . These seers (clairvoyants) and singers (clairchantants) are neither wise men nor prophets. They go to the fields like the others or sell their wares in the cities.[1]

Amrouche explains that these poets, *iferrahen*, 'those who rejoice, who give joy' sing of universal experience – of exile, death, God, love for the land, **68** sorrow and resignation.

These themes recur in contemporary Algerian poetry, transposed from the oral tradition to the written one, from Berber or Arabic to French. Thus, the generation of French-speaking Algerian writers, coming upon the literary scene at the end of the Second World War, far from bursting forth unattached, adds another link to a rich tradition of lyricism.

Modern Algerian writers of French expression have been termed 'the generation of 1954', for that date denotes the beginning of the struggle for independence,[2] yet the term is perhaps too narrow. A poet such as Kateb Yacine who was first marked by the bloody uprisings of Sétif and Guelma (two cities in Eastern Algeria) on 8 May 1945, also dwells upon earlier episodes in Algerian history, returning to his nation's pre-colonial past. In his novel *Nedjma*, published in 1956, Kateb Yacine states: 'We must put forward our Ancestors to discover the triumphant phase, the key of the victory denied to Jugurtha,[3] the indestructible germ of the nation torn between two continents.'[4] In addition, two Kabyle novelists, Mouloud Feraoun and Mouloud Mammeri have both sought to popularize a renowned bard of their Berber tradition, the nineteenth-century poet Si-Mohand-ou-Mohand.[5]

Reviewing the life and work of Si Mohand, as Mammeri has recently done, one develops a clearer understanding of Algerian preoccupations during the independence struggle, specifically the overwhelming sense of loss. Si Mohand, like his later counterpart, was marked by years of severe repression as French colonial authorities sought to break Kabyle resistance in the 1870s. At the time, the Berber population first experienced exile; men moved off the land to seek jobs, first in other parts of Algeria, finally abroad in France. Moreover, a society which formerly confronted problems involving a rigorous climate, a rigid honour code, now faced the challenge of a community in rapid mutation.

Against this backdrop, the poet Si Mohand, whose own family had been divested of its land, sung of his exile:

> I listened to the boat cry out
> My heart bled once again
> Oh, how separation does sow fear[6]

The poet regretted his lost paradise:

> I had a princely garden
> Jasmine and roses interspersed
> And flowers of all kinds
> I had encircled it with a closed wall
> Fed with water from the dam
> The door was made of planks and nails
> And then one day, it was a Sunday
> I went away
> The hawk arrived looking for pasture.[7]

This note of despair, the hollow sensation of viewing Eden ravaged, is the prelude to the outraged cry of revolt. Feraoun has described Si Mohand as the sage of a conquered people, for he preceded the generation that rebelled.

The theme of exile, however, is reasserted by the later Algerian poets, those embracing the revolution. Wandering through the ports of France, Mohammed Dib, in his solitude, also listens to the boats cry out:

> A ship that leaves shouts afar under the fog
> I turn in this city where the factories smoke
> Obstinately I try to remember, but what?[8]

Similarly, Malek Haddad, for whom exile is reflected in his use of the colonizer's language and customs as well as the physical separation from Algeria, writes:

> The city fears strangers
> She prefers her own ways
> I walk
> I shuffle along
> . . .
> I am a continent that dreams cast adrift.[9]

In contrast to Dib and Haddad, Amrouche is much less personal. Exile is a generalized *malaise*, the experience of the entire conquered nations:

> We no longer want to roam in exile
> In the present without memory and
> without a future.[10]

The refusal to remain in perpetual exile found expression following the upheaval of the Second World War. Once France emerged as a power whose strength could be tested by her colonial subjects, the nationalist spirit fostered by a minority in the twenties and thirties gathered momentum. In 1954 the barricades went up after a long period of discontent, misery, and injustice.

As a predecessor of the poetry of combat, Ismaël Aït Djafar's 'Complainte des mendiants arabes de la Casbah et de la Petite Yasmina tuée par son père',[11] captures the mood of this period between the two wars. Inspired by an incident in 1949 when a beggar pushed his daughter to her death under the wheels of a truck, the poem fuses an eye-witness account of violence – some would call it murder, others mercy – with the reassuring nursery rhymes taught in the French school system:

> But their tummies full, the children of Charlemagne
> Sing a song
> A song they learn at school . . .

The poet ironically addresses the long poem to Charlemagne, hero of his nation's conquerors. Thus, he juxtaposes the romanticized legends perpetuating the myth of French glory against the sordid squalor of the Casbah where barefoot beggars are by-passed by France's 'mission civilizatrice':

> Before she died
> little Yasmina
> slept there
> with her little papa
> who killed her
> simply
> brusquely
> with this paternal gesture
> not at all wicked
> of the toiling peasant
> conscientious
> who sows the little grain
> nine years old
> in the furrow
> of the wheels of a big truck passing
> and returning
> When the child appears
> tra la la
> and when the child disappears
> tra la la
> You don't know
> how that can enrage
> Those things that break our heart
> But no one cares . . .

Aït Djafar strikes a balance between violence – the result of the injustice of the adult world – and softness, contained in childhood innocence. For little Yasmina, death is a long sleep, a respite from misery. Similarly, the nursery rhymes, simple, soothing, and comforting, provide more fortunate children with a buffer against the harsh reality of adulthood. The poem compensates for its profusion of unchecked verbiage and a certain unevenness of tone by reaching the reader with sincerity and zeal. Once again, as in the songs of Si Mohand, we find a nostalgia for things past and a quest for beauty, love, and peace, in the face of present suffering.

When fighting broke out in the Autumn of 1954 and the colonized fought the colonizer in divided cities, Algerian poetry turned from the innocent victim of colonial injustice, Yasmina, to focus on the *maquisard*, the fighting man and his struggle. Yet the poets, each in his own way, nurtured memories of a lost paradise to be regained through victory. Anna Gréki, writing many of her poems while in prison in Algeria, evoked **71** her childhood home in the Aurès Mountains. Similar to the poets of the French Resistance, particularly Eluard, she remains committed to transmitting experiences anchored in reality and does so simply and directly. As a prisoner cut off from the outside world, she writes:

> No fire no love
> No sea no moon
> No flowers no children
> No peace no choice
>
> No right to the word
> No right to the song
> Each one in turn
> No right to our right[12]

Her poetry succeeds in re-creating lost joy and happiness for she, the prisoner, approaches and recaptures her paradise through memory. Moreover, in spite of present tensions and hatred, she commits herself to an idealized conception of fraternity and reaffirms her faith in the future:

> The future is for tomorrow
> The future is soon
>
> Beyond the walls closed like clenched fists
> Through the bars encircling the sun
> Our thoughts are vertical and our hopes
> The future coiled in the heart climbs towards the sky
> Like upraised arms in a sign of farewell
> Arms upright, rooted in the light
> In a sign of an appeal to love
> To return to my life
> I press you against my breast my sister
> Builder of liberty and tenderness
> And I say to you await tomorrow
> For we know
>
> The future is soon
> The future is for tomorrow.[13]

In spite of the revolutionary élan created by the intensity of the times, Anna Gréki remains a very personal poet, recalling her childhood, mourning her sweetheart killed in battle. In direct contrast to her work, we find the epic poetry of her contemporary, Nordine Tidafi. He chooses the collective voice and disappears as an individual to give voice to his people, his land:

> They have denied the certitude of our land
> They have destroyed Islam, its colour,
> fantastic tribes, to the shame
> that makes them live.

> They have denied the Vital Fire, our flag
> They have exiled the humble joys of our huts
> . . .
> Anonymous, reduced to hope, my People
> crosses the sun
> without witnesses,
> Awaited over there by misfortune.[14]

Thus, with varying degrees of intensity, the personal nightmare of the poet, as evoked by Gréki, and the collective anguish of the people, expressed by Tidafi, find expression during the years of combat.

United in a common struggle, Algerian poets of French expression share an arsenal of symbolic references: the sun, the night, the sea, mountains, trees, stars. These symbols drawn from nature reflect the hope that Algeria, threatened with destruction, will emerge from the struggle intact, to be reclaimed and restored by its people. Mohammed Dib, throughout his work, plays upon a homophone: mer/mère. Sea and Mother are intrinsically bound to one another, for both are life-giving as well as healing forces. Anna Gréki, Jean Sénac, Nordine Tidafi use the sun in much the same way. The tree, particularly the olive tree that dots the Mediterranean landscape, becomes *l'Arbre-Peuple* for Tidafi, the promise of roots for the entire nation. Jean Sénac, on the other hand, identifies the Algerian people with a tree deprived of roots, hence a mutilated nation. Finally, the star, which in Dib's universe links the poet to the cosmic forces, becomes the embodiment of Algeria itself to Kateb Yacine. Nedjma (star in Arabic) is the mysterious protagonist of Kateb's novels, plays, and poetry. First presented as a cloistered beauty attracting all men, Nedjma, the inaccessible dream, 'la femme fatale, stérile et fatale . . . ', she too dons a warrior's helmet and joins the *maquisards*.

Central to the poetry of colonized Africa, both north and south of the Sahara, is a nostalgia for unity in the face of chaos. Thus, two figures are ever present: the terrorist, who comes to destroy so that new structures may be created; the peasant, who attests to the continuity of life and who is waiting to repeat the age-old cycle of sowing and reaping. As bombs explode the figure of the terrorist looms large. In Kateb Yacine's universe, the terrorist lives the time that separates him from the explosion of the bomb:

> What is time
> But a bomb that delays
> and delays
>
> Time, this long lie
> Time, time that kills
> Time that until now killed us in silence

Time has found its bloody rhythm
Its gallop, its fury
Time, this long lie
. . .
Time was our ignorance
In the eyes of those who struggle
A false world shatters[15]

Sacrificing themselves so that their people may survive, these militants are:

Reduced to be nothing more than a living explosion
And who accepts to wait in the heart of the enemy
Our blood must light up and we must catch fire
So as to move the spectators
So that in the world finally eyes are opened
Not on our remains, but on the wounds
of the survivors.

The fellah, the Algerian peasant, is destined to survive and to restore unity and promote continuity. Dib, for whom the forces of nature heal and soothe, give voice to the promise of a new era by presenting the song of a peasant woman:

Strange is my country where
So many gusts are free
The olive trees move around me
And I sing:
– Burned and blackened earth
Friendly Mother
Your child will not remain alone
With the time that wounds the heart
Hear my voice
That carries through the trees
And makes the bulls bellow

This summer morning has arrived
I feel pregnant
Fraternal Mother
Women in their huts
Are waiting for my cry

I who speak, Algeria
Perhaps I am only the
Most banal of your women
But my voice will not stop
Calling the plains and the mountains

I come down from the Aurès Mountains
Open your doors

Fraternal wives
Give me fresh water
Honey and country bread.[16]

This song is an expression of a strong attachment to the land which, as all the symbolic references suggest – the olive tree, blackened earth, the Aurès – is Algeria. A universal theme, fraternity, is expressed by the woman who participates in life in all its forms by cherishing the earth, and giving her love and labour to it. The Fraternal Mother promotes love as well as procreation. We note that man is absent from the poem. No reference is made either to him or to his strength in the universe. It becomes clear in Dib's later, more symbolic, novels that the woman in Dib's world, because of her capacity both to dream and to create, is a more positive force than man. Her voice is anchored to reality, 'Hear my voice / that carries through the trees' and her words are simple and pastoral. They evoke the night, the mountains, the trees and the animals. Yet they are powerful, for her final words are in the form of a benediction: 'May your wheat grow, / May your bread rise too / And may nothing go wrong / Happiness be with you.'

Faith in the creative force of the word, a belief rooted in Algerian tradition, is reaffirmed by the poetry of Algerian resistance. As Dib proclaimed in 1957:

All the creative forces of our writers and artists, placed in the service of their oppressed brothers will make culture and the works it produces so many weapons of combat.[17]

However, we do find traces of ambiguity towards the role of the poet and the power of his word in time of actual combat. Sénac, for example, exclaims:

Why sing when we are menaced
By the death cry of innocence[18]

The problem is resolved for Sénac at least by strict adherence to Malek Haddad's tenet, 'Priority everywhere for useful songs'.[19] Thus, the conviction that poetry is a revolutionary act when the poet bears witness to the struggle of his brothers is reaffirmed:

I dared to speak!
I dared to greet you, sun!
My heart, I dared to live in the rhythm of your joy!
The cry of the tortured did not break my head!

Oh the world's injustice!
Nights on the entire surface of the body!
I dared in exile to name our suffering!

Oh brothers!
I lived through your dignity.
You gave us some inhabitable worlds.[20]

Once fighting ceased in 1962 and Algeria had won her struggle the poet was able to reassume his liberty of self-expression and to create a different song. As Dib explained:

... For several reasons, as a writer, my preoccupation at the time of my early novels was to merge my voice with the collective voice. Today that great voice is silent ... it was necessary to bear witness to a new nation and new realities. As these realities formed, I resumed my former attitude as a writer interested in problems pertaining to psychology, the novel, and style. The era of 'engagement' is over ... Literatures also serve their time.[21]

Expressing his own views, Dib did not voice a collective opinion. Malek Haddad, on the other hand, insists that peace has not come to Algeria, for the Arab world is still involved in conflict. In the Arab–Israeli war of June 1967 he reaffirmed his adherence to the struggle to liberate Palestine:

Gaza my soul where the Gazelle
Waits for the moonlight in the remembered garden
As long as the song is not at home
A strip of my flag is still to be woven.[22]

Similarly, many younger poets, those born in the 1940s, reflect Haddad's concern with a continuing struggle and view the Palestine issue as their own. A new review, *Promesses*, begun in 1969, has published a predominant number of poems treating the theme of war. Ahmed Aroua, who has published several collections of his poetry in Algeria, writes of the Egyptian school children of Bahr-el-Baqar.[23] Death, exile, prison, whether in the Middle East, or South-east Asia, or locked in the memory of the Algerian colonial experience, are themes that continually find expression in Algerian poetry today. This does not mean however that the Algerian poet avoids an introspective look at the realities of the post-colonial era. Among the younger poets' work we find criticism of the bureaucracy, outrage at the unfair treatment of women.[24] Rachid Boudjedra, in his collection *Pour ne plus rêver* (1965) questions the meaning of the revolutionary spirit in newly-independent Algeria.

Yet the primary focus of Algerian poetry of French expression in recent years has been upon the victory and the heroic warriors. As the poet Jean Sénac explains, 'still burning with the rhymes of combat, the young

poetry offers a fervent salute to the earlier woes while, at the same time, keeping a distance from the sorrow'.[25] To Sénac, poet of the 'generation of 1954', the new poetry is more enthusiastic, more constructive, more assured.

It is difficult to predict how far this revolutionary spirit will take its younger poets. For the majority of Algeria's people, the dove has folded her wings; peace has returned to the land. In Algeria today where a young population overflows streets named after fallen heroes, where whitened buildings sparkle in the Mediterranean sunlight, the ravaged paradise of Si Mohand-ou-Mohand has indeed been restored – if not in full, at least in good measure.

NOTES

1. Jean Amrouche, *Chants berbères de Kabylie* (Tunis, 1939, re-edited Paris: Charlot, 1947), pp. 40–1.
2. The phrase is attributed to Henri Kréa, Algerian poet and novelist. 'In my opinion and in that of the writers of the generation of 1954, the expression "Algerian writer" means in absolute terms that one has chosen the Algerian nation whatever one's racial origin, religious or philosophical belief may be.'
3. Numidian leader who rose against the Roman conquerors and was defeated by Marius, and killed 104 B.C.
4. Kateb Yacine, *Nedjma* (Paris, Seuil, 1956), p. 175.
5. Mouloud Feraoun, *Les Poèmes de Si Mohand* (Paris, Editions de Minuit, 1960). Mouloud Mammeri, *Les Isefra: Poèmes de Si Mohand-ou-Mohand* (Paris, Maspéro, 1969).
6. Mammeri, *op. cit.*, p. 51. All translations are provided by the author.
7. *Ibid.*, p. 275.
8. Mohammed Dib, 'Printemps', *Ombre Gardienne* (Paris, Gallimard, 1961), p. 52.
9. Malek Haddad, 'Début d'exil', *Écoute et je t'appelle* (Paris, Maspéro, 1961), p. 67.
10. Jean Amrouche, 'Le Combat algérien', in Denise Barrat, *Espoir et parole* (Paris, Seghers, 1963), p. 22.
11. Written in 1951, the poem appeared in *Les Temps Modernes*, No. 98, pp. 1227–52, was re-edited in 1963 by P. J. Oswald and was included in Jacqueline Lévi-Valensi and J. E. Bencheikh, *Diwan Algérien* (Alger, SNED, 1967), pp. 27–34.
12. Anna Gréki, 'Bonheurs interdits', *Algérie, Capitale Alger* (Tunis, P. J. Oswald, 1963), p. 38.
13. *Ibid.*, pp. 29–30.
14. Nordine Tidafi, 'La patrie totale', in Lévi-Valensi and Bencheikh, *op. cit.*, p. 204.
15. Kateb Yacine, 'La Bombe et le temps', in Barrat, *op. cit.*, pp. 92–4.
16. Mohammed Dib, 'Sur la terre, errante', *op. cit.*, pp. 23–5.
17. *Entretiens sur les lettres et les arts* (Rodez: Subervie, février 1957), p. 65. **77**

18. Sénac, *Matinale de mon peuple* (Rodez, Subervie, 1961), p. 39.
19. Haddad, *op. cit.*, p. 51.
20. Sénac, 'J'ai osé parler', *Matinale de mon peuple*, p. 86 reprinted in Lévi-Valensi and Bencheikh, *op. cit.*, p. 195.
21. Jean Chalon, 'Pour Mohammed Dib romancier algérien: le temps de l'engagement est passé', *Le Figaro Littéraire*, No. 946 (10 juin 1964), p. 4.
22. Malek Haddad, 'Je suis chez moi en Palestine', *Révolution Africaine*, No. 226 (12–16 juin 1967), p. 43.
23. Ahmed Aroua, 'Les écoliers de Bahr-El-Baqar', *Promesses*, No. 7 (mai–juin 1970), pp. 51–3.
24. See the poems of Youcef Sebti in Sénac, *Petite Anthologie de la jeune poésie algérienne: 1964–1969* (Alger: le centre culturel français d'Alger, 1969), pp. 30–40.
25. *Ibid.*, p. 8.

'Rara' Chants in Yoruba Spoken Art

Adeboye Babalola.

THE SOCIAL BACKGROUND OF THE CHANTS

Rara is one of the major types of Yoruba oral poetry. It consists of chanted poems with themes covering the entire range of the community's life and with a distinctive traditional stylistic device employed for the chanting.

In the course of my investigations about the *rara* tradition, my informants in several towns and villages in *Oyo* Province and Ibadan Province continually stressed to me the importance of grasping the distinction between *Esu-pipe* and *rara-sisun* and yet realizing the connection between these two traditional features of Yoruba life. They affirm that *rara-sisun* is an offshoot of *Esu-pipe* (literally: 'the calling of *Esu*') a term which refers to the recital of praise poems in adoration of *Esu*, the Yoruba trickster god. This recital is done in a voice style very much like that of normal speech. It is abrupt in its segmentation and it has a staccato ring. On the other hand, *rara-sisun* (literally, 'the singing voice recital of *rara*') is a term which refers to the chanting of *rara* poems for social merry-making in a voice style which certainly departs from that of ordinary speaking but falls clearly short of that of ordinary singing.

It is said that on social occasions, from as far back as the earliest period of the Yoruba kingdom, those who were experts in the recital of praise poems in adoration of *Esu* found a new outlet for their artistic energies in a new kind of poetic exercise without any implications of *orisa*-worship. The new outlet became known as *rara-sisun*.

A main source of stimulus for the new genre of Yoruba oral poetry was the desire of the King of *Oyo*, the Alaafin, to have in his palace a resident group of rhapsodists called *Arokin* whose duty would be 'to repeat daily in songs the genealogy of the kings, the principal events of their lives and other notable events in the history of the Yoruba country'.[1]

NOTE: As this article is a brief introduction mainly for non-Yoruba speakers it has been decided to dispense with accents in Yoruba. It is therefore regretted that the Yoruba is only a rough approximation.

The general term for the chanters of *rara* poems is *awon onirara*. Both men and women take to *rara* chanting and there is no clear predominance of either sex in the pursuit of the art. However, there is a marked difference between the mode for men and that for women. Many of my male informants explained that it was in their childhood that they started learning the art of *rara* chanting, in obedience to their parents, after the *Ifa* oracle had declared that it was to the guardian care of the god *Esu* that the Creator had assigned them from birth. From the age of five or six years, the *rara* pupil, if a boy, would be boarded with a master *rara*-chanter from whom he would learn the art by imitation and by memory work. Often the *rara* expert is also an acknowledged master in the art of *sekere* drumming and the boy learns everything about how to make *sekere* music² along with his learning of *rara*-chanting. He would stay as a pupil in the house of his master until late adolescence when, having achieved sufficient proficiency in what he had learnt, he would either abscond to set up practice on his own or take ceremonious leave of his master with a valedictory benediction given him on the occasion.

On the other hand, female *rara* chanters learn the art initially at home during their adolescence. The girl usually starts with repeated practices of the *rara* chants in praise of her father. She then moves on to *rara* chants on other themes including 'the bride's farewell to her parents' called *ekun iyawo*, i.e. the bride's tearful effusion. As a wife in her husband's home, the female *rara* chanter quickly learns to chant the *rara* poems in praise of her husband and his lineage, and she seizes the earliest opportunity on a festive occasion to give a solo performance of the chants to display her skill to her husband and his relations.

A distinct class of female *rara* chanters are those called *akunyungba* (literally: those who buzz or hum mellifluously). These are royal wives, especially in *Oyo* and *Iseyin*, who specialize in chanting *rara* poems on historical themes. They are reciters of the local chronicles in *rara* style. Sometimes their type of chanting is termed *yungba-kikun* – literally: 'sweet buzzing' in reference to the deep voice they use and the slow, long drawn out, flowing mode of their chanting which is devoid of any abrupt stops.

On the whole, the male *rara* chanters agree that the natural qualities of the female voice usually help the female *rara* chanters to give more melodious performances of *rara* chants than their male counterparts. But in overall rating of a given *rara* performance, much greater weight is given to extensiveness and accuracy of repertoire than to mellifluousness of voice.

For the men as well as for the women, *rara* chanting is not a full-time occupation but a side-line or a hobby. The women of course have their domestic chores to do, whilst the men are usually engaged in such full-time pursuits as cloth-weaving, farming, or tailoring. There is a traditional avoidance by *rara* chanters of activities such as hunting and the butcher's trade, in deference to the dictates of the god *Esu* from whose rites of worship, as has been earlier explained, *rara* chanting developed.

Remuneration for *rara* chanters includes not only plenty of food and drink on the festive occasion concerned but also considerable gifts of money. Where several *rara* chanters are assembled for performance, members of the audience indicate their high rating of an outstanding chanter by giving him extra special gifts usually in cash.

To attract the audience a *rara* chanter aspiring to receive the highest acclamation would almost invariably have *sekere* or *dundun* drum music accompaniment with his *rara* chanting performance.

At this juncture it is useful to point out that the *akigbe* is distinct from the *onirara*. The difference consists in the fact that whereas the *akigbe* is a *rara* chanter who is virtually a full-time resident employee of an *oba* or a *baale* or an *ijoye*, the *onirara* is an independent *rara* chanter who goes to perform at social gatherings to which he is either specially invited or self-invited.

Outer Form Characteristics of Rara *Chants*
The movement of *rara* chant is a halting forward movement without any suggestion of measured steps or balancement exercise. This is in clear contrast to *ijala* chant.[3]

The main feature which is present in *rara* rhythm but not in Yoruba prose rhythm is the abruptness, the jerkiness, the staccato effect, the marked segmentation; what makes H. Wolff describe *rara* as 'disjointed discourse'.[4] The rhythm-units in *rara* chant are much shorter than those of normal prose in Yoruba, e.g. conversation prose. This is not always evident, however, for the fast speed of chanting tends to obscure this feature in some cases.

Another characteristic feature worth mentioning is the sporadic elongation of final syllables in *rara* chant. This is a stylistic device employed for the purpose of rendering the chant more varied and less monotonous in sound. Finally, a word must be said here about the frequent tonal contrast at segment-ends in *rara* poems, as in other types of Yoruba poetry. For example, in the five lines quoted below, the tonal contrast at segment-ends is clearly indicated.

Olukekun[1] | *Alagbe*[2] | *ara Iwara.*[3]
Labala[4] | *olohundidun.*[5]
Alagbe[6] | *okoo Gbadejo.*[7]
Eni ti nsun rara fun San-an-ni[8] | *o ku.*[9]
Adepoju Alagbe[10] | *ti ti nsun rara*[11] | *ti nke s'Alaafin.*[12]
Aderounmu[13] | *baba Adedigba.*[14]

)

The segment-ends are numbered 1–14. There is tonal contrast between 1 and 2; 2 and 3; 3 and 4; 4 and 5; 5 and 6; 10 and 11; 11 and 12; 12 and 13; 13 and 14.

Inner Form Characteristics of Rara *Chants*
Idiomatic turns of expression are employed in great profusion in *rara* chants. These are dominated by the figurative use of words in metaphor, the use of imagery and symbolism in terse epigrammatic utterances and the use of appropriate phonaesthetic words. While these are featured in the representative examples of *rara* poems provided below, it is useful at this juncture to illustrate these points with particular reference to character sketches which abound in a *rara* chanter's repertoire.

In name-praising declarations that a certain person is to be recognized as a conqueror, a man of valour, a stern leader, here are some examples of figurative expressions employed by the *rara* chanters. Where the inference is not very clear, a word of explanation has been added.

> *Poogodo bi ogun ja'lu*
> (He who alone destroys his enemies like a full army plundering a town)
> *Ariwonmasojo (Ariwonmasa)*
> (He who sees his foes and does not flee)
> *Awotegunmafoya*
> (He who enters the battlefield and is not afraid)
> *Esuru o nii ya n'yan*
> (The *esuru* tuber is not for making pounded yam)

The key to the symbolism here is the fact that *esuru* is a certain variety of yam which is boiled and eaten in slices but is never pounded in a mortar for conversion into the popular Yoruba dish called *iyan*, because it is very brittle. By employing this symbolism, the poet intends to convey his opinion that just as people never contemplate pounding *esuru* even so would the hero's foes be well advised never to contemplate attacking him.

> *Ko to ni l'eru,*
> *Ti fi nta ni l'ori*
> (It isn't up to a standard load in weight,
> Yet it makes one's head to smart.)

The meaning of the imagery here is that the hero is a man of small build who inflicts acute pain on his enemies.

> *Ada nla abeekuyamu*
> (A big matchet with a broad handle)
> i.e. A mighty conqueror
> *Agba nla ojo ti ile eegun wo'le kerikeri*
> (A very heavy rain which drives the masquerader right indoors.)

82

i.e. An invincible man
Oka oju ona ti ile gurukoko
(A poisonous snake called *oka*, rearing its poised head
Over the massive coils of its spotted body)
Demudemu ko da'gbon;
Okuta le, oloko da a si.
(The palmwine tapster never taps a coconut palm;
A block of stone proves hard, therefore the farmer leaves it alone.)
i.e. A dreaded person given a wide berth by his foes.
Oloola ti mbe l'oke-odo,
Akomoloju akomolenu.
(Ritual face-cutter whose house is across the river
He who cuts marks on one's face and on one's mouth)
i.e. A slayer with the sword.
Apanikiotiotode
(He who puts one quite beyond self-control
Long before one is given any liquor to drink)
i.e. An awe-inspiring character

The following examples relate to figurative expressions used by *rara* chanters in saying that someone is a very important person of eminent status and mighty power.

Okansoso ibembe bori ilu
(A single *ibembe* drum drowns all the other drums.)
Igba abere ko t'oko;
Igba irawo ko t'osu.
(Two hundred needles do not weigh as much as a hoe;
Two hundred stars are not as bright as the moon.)
i.e. A multitude of the great man's foes
are not as powerful as the great man alone.
Ajanaku abirubamba
(An elephant with a bulky tail)
Erinfolawolu
(Elephant that walks into a town with dignity.)
Kuuku kan ko gba gunnugun
Igun ni baba eiyekeiye
(The vulture is never kept in a coop.
The vulture is the foremost of strange birds.)
Ogongo n'baba eiye
(The ostrich is the chief of birds.)
Otiti amiluwobiojo
(Quake-causing man who shakes the town
Like the rumbling in the sky before a rain.)
Ko si'le t'a a m'ewe
(There's no place where the *ewe* legume is not known.)
Eewo opolo ka'lu
(All over the town people know that the toad is not for human food.)
i.e. The great man is well known everywhere in town.
Efufulele nwon o s'eni aimo

(The wind is familiar to everybody.)
Oga n'kanun nse l'awujo okuta weere.
Okunrinn'ireke nse l'awujo eesun.
(Potash lumps rank highest among small stones.
The sugar cane is a leader among the grasslike plants.)
Alagbalugbu iroko ti if'ewon igba idi
(The great *iroko* tree that fastens a chain round its waist.)

The symbolism here consists in the signification of eminence among *iroko* trees. In traditional Yoruba society, a mighty *iroko* tree (African Teak) is believed to be inhabited by the local chief of spirits. Therefore the tree is revered and marked with a chain tied round its trunk.

Within the space limits of this article, these examples must suffice, leaving out figurative expressions for saying that a certain person is short or tall; fat or slim; quick tempered or gentle; pure-hearted or treacherous; generous or miserly; light-complexioned or dark-skinned; loud of voice or soft-spoken; wise or foolish; a farmer or a merchant; hardworking or slothful; beautiful or plain; agile or sluggish. There is also a profusion of imagery and symbolism in the poetic salutes to a medicineman, a talented dancer, a lover of liquor, a man of few words, and so on and so forth.

THE CONTENT OF THE CHANTS

The predominant theme in *rara* chants is the verbal salute which, coupled with benedictory utterances, is the ready resource of the *onirara* (the itinerant *rara* chanter) for the purpose of flattering an individual, arousing in him great pride in, and feeling of solidarity with, his ancestry and inducing him to lavish money on the performing minstrel. In these verbal salutes, personal names and agglutinate praise names occur in great profusion and this feature is what makes Hans Wolff describe *rara* as 'an artistic form of name calling'. Because of the pejorative connotation of the phrase 'to call one names', I would prefer to say that *rara* is 'an artistic form of name praising'.

In supplying examples of *rara* poems below, I have provided the original Yoruba text in only one or two cases for reasons of expedience. The emphasis is on Yoruba *rara* poems in English translation.

Poems of Flattery Specially Composed
to Fetch Lavish Money Presents from the Addressee

Olowolaiyemo

Olowolaiyemo, okunrin jeje abijakankan.
Baba ni'le, baba l'oko.
84 *Okansoso ajanaku ti nmi 'gbo aiye kijikiji.*

O ke ninu igbo, o d'eru ba ara ona.
O yo bi ojo, o d'efori fun omo oge.
O nf'igba bu sile, o tun nf'ase muti.
Olowolaiyemo nse nkan.
Olowolaiyemo nse nkan.
Eni ti ko dun mo k'o f'ori so'le.
Olowo ma nse nkan.

(*Olowolaiyemo*, the peace-loving man who fights hard.
A lord in town and a lord on the farm.
A single elephant that shakes the forests of the world.
His shout in the bush alarmed the people on the road.
He shines forth like the sun, and makes the ladies have acute headaches.
He gives out calabashes full of shilling pieces.
And drinks his liquor from a sieve.
Olowolaiyemo performs wonders.
Olowolaiyemo performs wonders.
Those who are displeased by this report
Should dash their heads upon the ground and bid goodbye.
The wealthy man performs wonders.)

Ladepo

Daranijo o!
Odekilekun o! Ladepo oo!
Odekilekun, okundedeteruteru.
Ajasa, adeilupewejo.
Abiringbere bi eni egbe ndun.
Egbe ko dun un, egbee re ni ko fee ki
Fulani se bi okunrin wolu.
Jakumo se bi ole wo 'jo eranko.
Labelabe yato ninuu koriko-odo yooku.
Babaa Rama, tire yato si tiwon.
Ti'e yato si t'omo elomii.

(Good man in society!
Ladepo, whose house fills up with guests
Soon after he comes home from abroad.
He whose baggage completely fills the spacious corridor.
Ajasa, whose magnetic personality
Attracts the youth in every town.
Man of slow steps, walking as if his ribs were bruised.
His ribs are quite all right, but his steps are slow
Because he's trying to avoid his equals in the streets.
The Fulani herdsman walks into our town
Like a sick man, feverish and feeble.
The jackal acts the sluggard
As he joins a crowd of animals.
The *labelabe* is quite distinct among the grasses on the river bank.
Father of Rama, your character is different from 'theirs'.
Your generosity is nonpareil.)

Verbal Salute to the Hospitable Man

Young man as handsome as an antelope.
A fine stalwart worthy of the Balogun chieftaincy.
He who spends lavishly on entertaining guests,
As if he has a mint in his own house.
5 His style of boundless hospitality
Is not attempted by the white men in our land,
Lest they find themselves landed in the red.
He who stores tomorrow's drinks in his house today,
Filling every room in the house with drinks.
10 He who stores tomorrow's food in his house today,
Filling every room in the house with food.
The great uplifter,
Who made his barber rich enough to buy a horse.
The great protector,
15 Who clothes a minstrel with a robe.
He does not avoid visitors.
He sees a minstrel coming and waits at home for him.
He wears voluminous robes
Which make him appear puffed up
20 Like one wearing several clothes in the harmattan.
He quickly bends double
To charge full force against a foe.
It is as hard to injure him
As it is to trim the branchlets of an *ako* tree.
25 One would think thrice
Before one dares to deal him any blow,
While at work together on the farm.
Slender though he is, 'Toughness' is his name.
He quickly collects himself, after a fall.
30 Various foodcrops flourish on his farm:
Maize, mother to our *eko* dish,
And the black-eyed bean, father to our food called *olele*.
He who dishes 'it' out with a calabash.
He who shares out his money with a large calabash.
35 A cocoyam planted on a marshplot's edge
Never suffers from poverty.
A citizen of *Ife* Town who has blood ties with the King, the *Ooni*,
Never suffers from penury.
I know that since I'm now your guest,
40 I shall never again experience poverty.
To you I have fled, for sure refuge.
On your back I have climbed, for real security.
The *ivere* climbing plant is never thrown off by its supporting tree.
Without the *tagiiri* fruit, we cannot 'shave' a hide.
45 Without you in society, all our labours are of no avail

Verbal Salute to Olukekun Adepojumi[5]

Olukekun[a] 'Poju.[b]
Aderounmu.[c]
Death having killed the owner of a farm hut, the farm becomes desolate.
Father of *Adedigba.[d]*
5 *Olukekun Alabi,[e]* citizen of *Iwara.*
Alagbe,[f] a slave of *Ogunrinde.*
'Bayo, father of *'Lalounpe.*
He who has a pair of farmer's shorts well made for him.
But wears it for purposes other than farm work.
10 He whose employment is lips-using work[i] which he clearly prospers in.
He strolled along quietly
On h s way, past the backyards of the houses.
He went to give due food to the divinities
On the way to the potters' clay quarry site.
15 *Aderounmu,* father of *Adedigba.*
He thought this out, he thought that out, he thought out many things.
He sold this, he sold that, he sold the other one.
He thought this out, he thought that out, he thought out many things.
This reputed man thought out equivalents in two languages.
20 *Alagbe.*
Olukekun.
Aroolola.[j]
You thought of what to do to make a mark.
A resolute person turns deaf ears to contrary opinions.
25 *Pojumi,* a resolute person
Must not heed such.
Adebayo, father of *'Lalounpe.*
His mother engaged in the dyeing trade.
This reputed *Olukekun.*
30 He was fond of saying: 'When a woman decides to stop being a man's
     mistress she invariably exaggerates his faults'.
Aderounmu, father of *Adedigba*
Olukekun, Aiabi, citizen of *Iwara*
Alagbe a slave to *Ogunrinde.*
35 *Adebayo* offspring of 'Mother Dyer'.
Adepojumi.
Offspring of the *Osorun* chief of *Eran* Town.
Olukekun.
'When a woman decides to stop being a man's mistress,
40 She invariably exaggerates his faults.'
Women who live as mistresses are real bounders.
Adepojumi, when they want to break with their men,
They never do so quietly.
Olukekun.
45 A mistress spins one like a top and rains abuses on one,
Saying that one's mouth resembles that of a horse.
Oribolawa, offspring of *Alalaekun.*
Olukekun, 'It is the culprit who goes about canvassing for favours.
A crime of which one is innocent never ruffles one.

87

50 If you have no well-placed man to hang upon
You put all your energy into your work.'
Aderounmu, father of *Ade*.
Aderounmu, father of *Adedigba*.
A man who answered to the name 'Sanusi'
55 Although he did not profess the Islamic faith.
Husband of 'Mother from Ibadan'.
Alagbe, husband of *'Gbadejo*.
May you have good fortune in your heavenly home!ᵏ
'Poju, may you encounter good fortune wherever you go.
60 Good fortune will meet you often.
Ill luck will steer clear of you.

Verbal Salute to Gbarogbola Alumu⁶

I *Akande*, father of *Adepele*.
Emmanuel *Ayinde*, do pay due homage to my father.
When the earthworm pays homage to the earth,
The earth opens up for it.
5 I pay due homage to *Gbarogbola Sakunileke Alamu*.
Each one of us has in his home some lord and master whom he reveres.
Gbaragbola's lord and master is in the king's official residence
Alamu was fond of saying, 'The time for merry-making is after feeding.
'A hungry man is an unhappy man,' *Aroola Sakunileke*.
10 He who with *aro* cymbals made for himself a name.
Gbarogbola whose *aro* cymbals regularly clanged merrily in the palace.
Gbaragbola Sakun ileke Alamu.
He it was who gave birth to *Onibonoje*.
Ayilara who scarifies his offspring with red hot iron.
15 *Ayinde*, man fond of saying, 'Children are to the credit of the dirty wife
But for the children she has born, she would be driven from her
husband's house.'
Offspring of *Agarabiawu* who often said 'The ruler of a town
Would not like to see the town deserted.'
Agarabiawu continued, 'It's some of the inhabitants who do things
tending towards that.'
20 He who thrived before the very eyes of his detractors.
In the sight of his detractors he went for a ride on his white horse.
'The scornful man will have nothing else to do but scorn.'
I am the Song of *Gbaragbola Sakun ileke Alamu*.
Wait!
25 Owner of a *koso* drum of compact size.
Heir to the throne, *Oyindaola SoladEmi*, son of *Olojoibi*.
Siyanbola, the leader, father of *Gbadegesin*.
'Twas on the death of the panther
That the lot fell on the leopard to uphold the house.
30 King, son of *Abiodun*, the leader praisenamed *Wolounmole*.
Elephant of a son, first born of a great father.
Solademi son of *Olojoibi*.
88 Owner of a *koso* drum of compact size, father of Mojoyin.

Bearer of praisenames resembling those of his grandfather.
35 Elephant of a son, he who was born with a frown on his face.
Solademi!
He was fond of saying that there were seven things
Which differed in size one from another.
You ask me 'What are they?'
40 Seven big ants put together are not as big as one cockroach.
Seven cockroaches put together are not as big as one waxbill.
Seven waxbills put together are not as big as one fowl.
Seven fowls put together are not as big as one goat.
Seven goats put together are not as big as one horse.
45 Seven horses put together are not as big as one elephant.
Seven elephants put together are not as big as *Igbadi* Hill.
Four hundred and forty persons put together,
O Owner of a *koso* drum of compact size, Leader, son of *Atoba*
Shall never be as big as *Ladigbolu Akanbi.*
50 *Woluunmole!*
Head of the hunters, O king, son of *Abiodun*
Elephant of a son, firstborn of a great father.
Solademi son of *Olojoibi.*
He made a certain statement in passing.
55 Outstanding king, son of *Olatunbosun.*
All of you the *élite*, and the generality of the citizens,
Didn't you mark it?
Ask me, say, 'What did *Gbadegesin*'s Father of *Oyo* say?'
He said, 'The needle will pass through the gate of ropes
60 'Before it becomes completely blocked.
'When *Ladigbolu Akanni* is already dead
'Then will power pass into the hands of Councillors.'
Owner of a *koso* drum of compact size, our Leader,
You had a vast circle of loyal informants.
65 A Field Marshal who never went to war!

A Bride's Valediction to Her Family

Give me my share of your benediction before I depart.
Glory of the street, give me my share of your benediction before I
    depart
Member of my lineage, father of *Adeyemo.*
Glory of the street, father of *Adetoro.*
5 The king's firstborn son, the snail does not dance to the *sekere* music
O lion of a man, the chameleon does not dance to the *goba* music
Firstborn son of *Aremu Adeleokun Ilumo Afiikoode.*
Glory of the street, my father, he's the one who will escort me on my
    way.
Song : (Chorus to the chant)
    Father will escort me on my way,
10 O *Ajibike.*
    Father will escort me on my way.
Member of my lineage,
Who rides on horse-back scattering dust about,

89

Glory of the street, father of Adetoro.
15 If we are considering royal connections,
Citizen of *Osun Ido*,
Ajibike, our father has many royal links.
Father of *Adeyemi*, father of *Adeyemo*.
Father of Adebiyi, father of Adetoro.
20 He whose house is crowded with relations.
Lion of a man in whose house every caller is fully fed.
Folarin, our father, he who is welcomed home by thronging crowds.
It's he who will escort me on my way.
Glory of the street, my father, he will escort me on my way.
25 Member of my lineage, father of *Adeyemo*.
Father of Adebiyi, father of Adetoro.
Lion of a man, the chameleon does not dance to the *goba* music.
Firstborn son of *Aremu Adelokun Olumo Afiikode*.
Song: (Chorus to the chant)
He will escort me on my way.
30 He who clothes both daughter and mother,
He will escort me on my way.
Member of my lineage, who rides on horseback scattering dust.
He who clothes both daughter and mother.
Ajibike, I have clothed my mother.
35 I say my father will escort me to my husband's home.
He who clothes daughter and mother, I say I am ready to leave.
Son of *Mimoloso*,
I wish to be on my way.
Son of *Wojuola*, husband of *'Peode*.
40 I say my father will escort me to my husband's home.
My father who goes to the market and returns home with a load of
things.
He will escort me on my way.
I say if you ask a masquerader to accompany me,
The masquerader will surely leave me at some stage,
45 And return to his abode in heaven.
If you say it's an *orisa* that will accompany me,
The *orisa* will surely leave me at some stage,
And return to his abode in heaven.
Why not say it's my head that will escort me to my husband's home.
50 My head will go with me right into my allotted room.
It is one's head that goes with one to one's matrimonial home.
Mother of *Gboyeola*, I wish to be on my way.
Kanyinola, daughter of *Omowaare*.
Kanyinola, daughter of him who owns sixteen horses,
55 Eight of which feed in the stalls, while the other eight feed at large.
Daughter of him who owns some mules.
Ojuola, husband of *Monike*, *Aboogidi*.
Alao, don't trample on me with your horse's hooves
O *Aboogidi*.
90 60 He who goes to the market and brings home slaves

Has been riding about on a young elephant without treading any one to
death.
Omotoso.
Ojuola, husband of *'Peode.*
Your majesty, *Alao,* father of *Lawani.*
65 *Alao,* to whom people flee for refuge and give themselves to him.
Wearer of elaborate robes appreciated from afar,
Husband of *Olubimpe.*
Ayanlola Alajiki,
Star artist in the dance, husband of *Oniyemoja.*

Benedictions

All the good things you think about and wish to have
Shall indeed be yours in God's good time.
In trying to solve the problems in your life,
You shall never find yourself at your wits' end.
5 Your home shall never drive you from itself.
Your money-earning way shall never beat you up.
That rascally gnome by name The Snatcher Elf
Shall never snatch from you that which is yours.
You shall not fall and thereby leave this world.
10 The ground you tread shall ever lie flat for you.
By your work you shall always earn good pay.
You shall never earn hot coins or notes.
Extravagance shall never capture you
Nor shall you ever be compelled
15 To spend your money on defraying costs in court,
Or paying fines imposed on you by law,
Or making good some loss from fire or storm.
Such baneful waste shall never be your lot.
You shall always be invisible
20 To wicked people who would do you harm.
Their trap of tangled ropes shall never capture you.
The food you buy shall be to your delight.
You shall never lack good friends on whom to call
And you shall always have your own dear home.
25 Your house shall never prove too hot for you
Nor shall it ever collapse upon your head.
Never shall your wife decide to part from you
And never shall she have to call for help
From priest or medicineman at her childbirth.
30 When you have fed and felt full-satisfied
Whatever remnant food you then do have
Shall not be wasted,
But shall feed the offspring of your loins.

NOTES

(A) *Explanatory Notes on Salute to Olukekun Adepojumi*

(*a*) *Olukekun:* The literal meaning of this personal name is 'The prominent man has cut a path through the ocean'. The deeper meaning is that the father of the child so named is hereby recording the fact that he has had great difficulties to surmount before having the baby boy.

(*b*) *'Poju:* This is an abbreviation of '*Adepojumi*' a personal name which means literally 'There are too many crowns for me'. It signifies that the child's father considers the child one too many. See Dr O. Johnson, *The History of the Yorubas* (London, 1921), p. 82.

(*c*) *Aderounmu:* The name means 'He who comes and enters into possession of a lot of property'.

(*d*) *Adedigba:* 'My crowns now number two hundred', i.e. 'I am blessed with very many children'.

(*e*) *Alabi:* A praise name; an attributive name, meaning 'He whose birth enriches his parents by providing the first male child.'

(*f*) *Alagbe:* An attributive name. 'Baby who enriches everyone who carries it'.

(*g*) *'Bayo:* abbreviation of '*Adebayo*', 'Child who arrives and finds joy in the family.'

(*h*) *'Lalounpe:* the full form of this name is '*Olalohunpe*' meaning 'Child who has everything she wants'.

(*i*) *lips-using work:* i.e. quasi-professional chanting or singing.

(*j*) *Aroolola:* the full form of this name is '*Arorolola*' meaning 'Honour sets people's tongues wagging''.

(*k*) The person addressed is now deceased.

(Space does not permit the author to provide further explanatory notes here.)

(B) *General*

1. S. Johnson, *History of the Yorubas* (Lagos, 1898), p. 58.

2. *Sekere* music is produced by the skilful jingling of empty, dried gourds of various sizes bedecked almost completely with strings of cowries. There are three types of gourds (termed respectively *iya-ilu sekere, pepa* and *omole*) in a standard set of *sekere* musical instruments. To these are added a pair of *aro* which are metal objects resembling magnified cowries, each containing one or two musket balls.

3. See S. A. Babalola, 'The Characteristic Features of Outer Form of Yoruba Ijala Chants', *ODU* Volume 1, Numbers 1 and 2 (July 1964 and December 1965).

4. H. Wolff, '*Rara: A Yoruba Chant*', *Journal of African Languages*, Volume 1, Part 1 (1962), pp. 45 ff.

5. The subject of this verbal salute is a master chanter of *rara* poetry, a man under whom the chanter successfully pursued his pupillage as a *rara* chanter.

6. From a *rara* chant transcribed from tape-recording of a performance given by *Ogunsina Ayinde* of *Ile Alaro* in *Oyo Tow*.

The Universe is my Book: Lenrie Peters

Edwin Thumboo

Much of *Satellites* is informed by a seriousness of purpose derived from a belief that poetry has a function, one made especially urgent by the compulsions of modern society, the 'life with Figures / or chanting laws' (p. 19).[1] Peters sees the intuitive life – upon which the growth of the individual largely depends – as increasingly assailed by 'statistics, graphs and charts'. In the face of an over-assertive intellect man suffers, *inter alia*, a retreat of the body's thinking. This weakening of links between emotion and intellect is a major theme of twentieth-century literature, one which Léopold Senghor exploited by giving prominence to claims regarding the unique nature of the African personality when he worked out the founda-tions of negritude.[2] To some extent the position Peters takes is in the tradi-tion of Senghor's well-known stand except that he is mainly concerned with the dissociated sensibility as a contemporary problem.

Peters decided, quite rightly, that the poet, moved by a particular combination of interests, educates through offering a positive resistance to this encroachment by the intellect. Those of his poems devoted to this theme provide a view of his essential thinking on the function of the poet, of language, and of crucial directing energies. However, Peters is not a didactic poet; if he were, the level of performance in *Satellites* would be appreciably lower, and the complexity, the excitement of ideas in Poem 36 and elsewhere, less admirable. Nor is he anti-intellectual; he rejects the abstract, the calculating, on account of their depressive power.

It is useful to note the care with which Peters approached his responsi-bilities. Poem 9 is an extremely revealing document for this purpose:

> I want to
> drag you out
> shake your eyes
> open with pictures
> sounds and words
> compel your imagination.   (p. 18)

93

Peters is recalling the poet as educator, a role no longer fashionable. In an important sense, poetry is a social activity, written 'not / for strangers / and Mars', but an immediate audience. There is something old-fashioned in this, though we should not for this reason judge it inadequate. Nor do we detect any improper presumption, as the role receives extensive support from traditions of African vernacular poetry, except that in them the primary interest is the collective, not the individual, imagination.

It follows that for Peters the nature of his audience affects whatever assumptions he may make about the purpose of his poetry. Should he write for readers in Africa, or for those abroad who, better acquainted with poetry in English, expect a certain degree of sophistication? Artistic integrity is important. It is patently dangerous for an African to write with his eyes on the overseas market. He would then want to please non-African readers, catering for special expectations at the expense of his vision: 'you can ruin your art / Trying to please them' (p. 26). Peters mentions Yevtushenko, Stalin, and censorship, intimating that there the restraints, however severe, were clear, and admitted a straightforward confrontation. As the state supervises artistic functions, a writer who asserts his freedom does so at considerable personal risk. The gesture ceases to be purely a question of artistic integrity. But 'Here you write as you please'. However, the apparent freedom, while liberating, could turn sinister if it encouraged the second-rate, the questionable:

> Here you write as you please
> But need a talent without music
> Mind without ideas or desires
> A bleeding ignorance of form
> And language of obscurity
> Then you are well mounted
> And may even get published . . .　(p.47)

The lack of proper standards for the judgement of poetry – prose is less problematical, or problematical in a different way – affects the value of writing.[3] What Peters lists – ideas, forms, language – while overlapping is fundamental.

Their practical consequences make Peters's views important. He could not have escaped being aware that the strength of a poet depends equally on what he has to offer and the means at his disposal to accomplish a full communication. The way he describes the process – 'drag you out', 'compel your imagination', 'Drag you to / your knees till / you sniff' – is indication enough. Creative energies must be matched by stylistic resources and both brought together in the revealing intimacy of a potent vision, a **94** particular reading of experience.

As one would expect, the first demands and inspires a special interest in words. However valuable the vision, whatever the body of insight, ideas remain inaccessible but for the agency of words. The crusade is endless:

> Words are cumbersome elusive
> sophisticated in their demand of skill
> Vulgarized by loquacity. (p.59)

It is worth stressing that the challenge exists for Peters as a poet, not as an African poet, a discrimination which helps to rebut those who insist that there are barriers rather than inhibitions obstructing the movement of a language across cultural frontiers. Whether the result is pillage or poetry depends on the poet's skill, the extent to which the subject is taken into his thinking. As Peters put it 'I / focus / through words' to embody what 'lies / behind the truth / with infinite clarity' (p. 19). The practice of Peters's poetry is eminently sensible: the language is there to exploit.

Colonizing a language demands an application that goes beyond an appreciation of its more solid virtues. Fresh nuances inspired by the familiar and that brand of thinking which is essentially exploratory both fall outside and prove too complex for habitual patterns of language:

> Thought ⸜
> concreted, emancipated
> in feeling not by word. (p. 58)

Obviously, the more transparent the medium, the less resistance offered to the message. Peters does not, however, deliberately keep the two separate; in a number of the poems discussed later, message and medium become co-extensive, as they should be. The perspective he seeks, one in which neither medium nor message gets neglected, is linked to the kind of poems – of which Poem 36 is the outstanding example – which he wants to write. That is the ultimate aim, a poem in which matter and style fuse to create a permanent, yet continually expanding, metaphor.

But creative powers of this dimension result from an accumulation of small, even painful, discoveries. In the Mbari volume Peters was already getting acquainted with the discipline and the opportunities offered by the quatrain.[4] Another example of what he sought is provided by the rhythm of ideas. It is possible to talk of two rhythms. In one, syllables, stressed and unstressed, provide a verbal flow to the language; the other offers a flow of ideas, as they lead into each other and mesh. Ideally, the two rhythms co-exist. Peters is able to manage both simultaneously, **95** though we find instances where he concentrates on one, as in this stanza of Poem 11:

> Atmosphere!
> meadows, trees ripe aflame
> cattle netted by highways;
> masked highways fleeing past
> adverts, lights, cables
> Noise, squeaking, breaking
> grinding heaving, swearing whining
> fleeing confusedly into darkness, deep night.

The lines move on the level of implication, the ideas generating a rhythm working towards a unique coherence. Each phrase or image, constructs or recalls a mood, a feeling, a historical or literary parallel. The very close texture which results is further intensified by words with a basic, almost rudimentary meaning: 'aflame', 'netted' and 'fleeing'. Peters is able to achieve a subtle and penetrating statement, touching those areas of our sympathy which lie almost on the borders of the subconscious.[5]

Other characteristic features, ranging from biblical allusions to the extremely delicate recovery of a scene[6] are considered in the discussions that follow. The example adduced above is sufficient to show a consistent devotion to procuring the elements of style.

The import of Peters's emphasis on firm personal conviction and the necessity for self-understanding is seen in its proper light when we recall pioneer poetry, especially its tendency to confine itself to the superficial attractions of a theme. A comprehensive statement is achieved by penetrating a subject to reach its limits,[7] an undertaking requiring insight, resilience and strength of an unusual kind. Peters seeks to avoid cursory treatment through a commitment of his full personality; for him a poem is nothing if not the:

> throwback of
> my vision   (p. 18)

This vision, whether inspired by 'sunsets' or 'mornings', the corruption or the infinite promise of man, while it owes its ultimate expression to language, depends equally on the unifying capacities at the poet's disposal, a point established by the very first piece in *Satellites*. A modest, unpretentious poem, it carries an account of Peters's initiation. While the whole conceptual development is nowhere near Christopher Okigbo's performance in *Heavensgate* or *Limits*, the purpose and progression are recogniz-

ably similar:

> Run me through
> with odiousness, Politics
> Isms, deceits, vanities
> yet leave me the colour of truth   (p.3)

Elsewhere in the poem the images of invading locusts (with their biblical associations), muscles tightening in agony on 'mountain shoulders', 'Ecstasy and passion' with 'giant wings', speak of the protagonist's terror and the desolation and torment of the earth. Man partakes of earth's passion, is subjugated, driven to 'Heinous laughter', into destructive isolation before discovering that 'Heaven' lies within rather than without. Clearly this baptism of suffering – it is no less – forms a turning point on account of the understanding it brings:

> Heaven is in
> my blade of grass
> my fire to survive
> to cherish survival   (p. 3)

Discovery of faith ensures survival and leads to a secure possession of the truth. 'Politics / Isms, deceits, vanities': the list reads like the key terms of an updated morality. They are the temptations, the digressions, but he takes himself through:

> I gasp with possibilities
> only; I believe,
> shout; I believe!
> I BELIEVE.   (p. 3)

The symbolism of light and darkness, Christian and explicit, charts the poet's constant raids into the inarticulate. It especially recalls Poem 34 in which suffering is a prelude for understanding. What matters here, however, is the arrival at conviction, a conviction essentially part of that larger, declared purpose of moving and extending minds. It is inherent in Peters's argument that the more ample the individual life, the greater its psychological weight.

   Peters is unusually clear about his intentions, Even if he does not quite work them into poetry, he remains aware of the difficulties underlying any attempt to announce basic intentions. He is conscious of the need both to be understood – which explains the direct mode of address – and to elicit and sustain a sufficient response. None the less we notice a gap between his good and poor poems. Those devoted to poetry and the poet, while giving the impression of making poetry out of ideas, remain too **97** single-minded to be more than satisfactory. Their subject matter belongs firmly to the province of prose and criticism, from which they cannot be easily shaken free. We note the verbal support – 'Cannonade of wings / in motion', 'A bleeding earth / ferments in agony' – but remain convinced that the dominant energies of his style are but partially engaged. The majority of his poems with specifically African themes seem open to the same censure.

What we miss is that sense of language assembled under the pressure of creative intelligence which Peters achieved to a limited extent in Poem 18:

> The first rose of the season
> Yellow pink or red
> With petals neatly curled
> Like the foetal head
> Inside an egg
> Hinting layer by layer
> Under the living dew-drops
> At the perfect balance
> Of that which is to come
> In the full power
> Of subdued fragrance.   (p. 35)

The simile is left behind once the identification of rose and egg is accomplished; the movement is fermented on two levels with each strengthening the other. The evocative clarity with which the unfolding life is felt through the mind's ability to grasp parallels is truly striking. From line five, the drift of thought includes both rose and egg, kept together by the double application of a number of phrases: 'neatly curled', 'Hinting layer by layer', 'living dewdrops', 'perfect balance', and 'subdued fragrance'. Although Poem 18 is a minor piece, it is a significant demonstration. Only a handful of African poets writing in English can muster such constructive power. Where this power is lacking, the poetry suffers a loss of intensity. In *Satellites* the poems on broad African themes are underwritten. They are not undertaken with Peters's characteristic utterance and merely confirm that the subject had little power to move him. Perhaps Africa as a subject proves too large unless personalized by and engaged through elements of the kind offered by *négritude*.

Senghor delivers a new humanism out of the African virtues, Peters sees them as elements feeding his power as a poet. Senghor's view is perilously close to propaganda, though Senghor himself was too skilful a poet to be guilty of that. Peters, on the other hand, was never exposed in quite the same way. By making them part of his stylistic equipment, the thrusts of the African inheritance, the habit of seeing things as representational and **98** so forth, were means to an end, rather than ends in themselves.

Although the attributes of the *African Personality* got absorbed into his creative personality, the power to appropriate and synthesize is not evident in the poems about Africa. We are struck by a lack of vitality. Poem 45, about post-independent Africa, never really comes alive. Peters starts with the primaeval unity of Africa: 'In the beginning / one voice / one cry / one promise'. A series of quick phrases takes us through the period of colonial rule to the advent of politicians who inspired and led the people out of their pan-African suffering. Only rarely is the narrative relieved, as when he comments bitingly that the politicians 'beg in style' or 'We shall abolish / the Tse Tse fly' or 'the death rate stayed alive'. So the panorama unfolds: political hypocrisy, indiscretions, the new burden of suffering, the formation of the OAU, the arrogance of Nkrumah, the cold war (Russians versus Chinese), UDI, ending tamely with:

> In the end
> Smith slipped through the net.   (p. 89)

Embedded in a plethora of facts is the dialogue between peasant and politician which disclosed the frustrated hope, the harsh treatment of Africans by Africans:

> But excuse me, sir;
> We're free.
> Why do we have to beg?
> Industrial development
> Dams, factories, the lot –
> change the face of the Continent.
> 'I see
> But my children –
> beg pardon Sir,
> will they go to school?'
> Later!
> 'Will they have food to eat
> and clothes to wear?'
> Later I tell you!
> 'Beg pardon Sir;
> a house like yours?'
> Put this man in jail.   (p. 84)

But even here the appeal is to the betrayal implicit in the social, economic and political realities which emerged after independence. The subject is legitimate, perhaps too much so, as its inherent power to secure assent reduces the need to write creatively. What appeal it enjoys is from elements that are not specifically literary.

The conclusion is exceptional:

There is hunger and sickness
in the land
I say there is a cauldron burning
on that plain
red earth, red vengeance
all aflame
must it be born in vain?
I carry a ball of fire
on my head
and cannot put it down
I pray for rain, for vital floods
to come again. (p. 89)

The yearning and the suffering of Africa and the voice of the poet merge.
Peters picks his words carefully: 'hunger', 'sickness', 'burning', 'earth',
'vengeance', 'aflame', 'rain' and 'floods'. He has, after all, made it a point
to study them. These are elemental, close to the situation he describes.
Both 'rain' and 'floods', especially, suggest cleansing and fructifying
powers. The lineal arrangement provides a broad rhythm within which the
short lines move in subtle variation; the images of destruction and purification make the genuineness of his agony clear:

The oceans lick my toes
rush downhill with time
I burn in my heart,
in that desolate plain
raped, plundered, decimated . . .
Unity come back
embrace it
hold it
as in the beginning
In the end
One voice
One people
out of the dark struggle. (p. 90)

Compared to the best, as a group the poems on Africa are inferior.
Somehow his perceptions fall negligent, his intelligence and vigour are
withheld from the poetry. That capacity to simplify and yet retain the
essentials, loses its force. The poems confirm that the specific situation,
the specific experience is what best inspires Peters; his lyrical gift comes to
full power. When he steps out of first-hand experience, his style loosens
rapidly. The expansiveness of public themes does not offer inducements
to the upper reaches of his style.

As a whole, the nature poems are more resourceful. Autumn, hovering
100 between ripeness and decay, with its stark beauty, is the favourite season.[8]

It reaches into Peters, 'burns' and makes his skin 'taut with expectation', summons up an immense sorrow out of which arise positive assertions:

> Great trees in transit fall
> are made naked in langour of shame
> solitary like actors on a stage
> like stars, orphans, celebrities,
> politicians, uncomfortably mysteriously
> like you and me.   (p.4)

The gathering of feeling, the transition from the sheer sensational brightness of autumn – '*burns* me with / primaeval *fire*' – through to the seasonal death implicit in 'transit', 'naked' and 'solitary', possesses a sad, tensed, precision against which he gambles the recrudescence of passionate feeling:

> But I will not mourn the sadness.
> I will go dead-leaf gathering
> for the fire in a slice of sunlight
> to fill my lungs with odours of decay
> and my eyes with mellowed rainbow colours.   (p. 4)

It is the same 'primaeval fire', curiously heartening, which will consume the remains of autumn. For out of death comes life: 'I will go . . . and listen . . . and hold . . .'

> Then I will love
> Yes love; extravagantly.   (p. 5)

The wonders of autumn, its decay paradoxically carrying the promise of new life, enable a metaphysical leap from sorrow to wonder and hope. Peters's response is poignant, complete, and adult, taking him beyond sadness to a positive life-force. The whole weight of the experience is in fact heightened by a descriptive delicacy that is found elsewhere only in a number of poems by Dennis Brutus.

Peters's contact with nature is intimate: her rhythms and images, her sensual appeal, continue to identify and clarify his thoughts. But despite his recognition of her miracle, her formidable presence, he resists any mystical worship of nature. She functions as an auxiliary language, conveying his feelings, his inner life.[9] In Poem 7, his response is almost subcutaneous – landscape and fields, 'grey with corn', the rhythms in the colours of twilight, the whole physical scene, work on his mind. Impressions multiply, are associated with life to yield an enlarged context which

in turn affects the mood of the landscape. As a result of the 'Full disorder
... Being in revolt' the

> Evening comes prematurely, unexpectedly
> feet aching with years
> broken by retreating clouds of sunshine
> youth now past the Meridian. (p. 14)

What he perceives modifies what he thinks; what he thinks modifies what
he feels in a conjunction which calls forth his whole personality:

> Clouds waving into and out of distance
> beckon obscurely with limpid hints
> tints on leaves, shades of feeling
> majesty of knowing, perception. (p. 14)

The last line is crucial to our understanding, for the changes – 'limpid
hints / tints on leaves' – are equally changes within his mind. They make
up the 'majesty of knowing'; his feelings not only provide the material;
they extend and shape the accompanying thought as well.

The ambit of these poems is larger; Peters achieves a resonance through
metaphors having arms in both worlds. We respond to the poignant life
which surfaces in them, that sense of tragedy and joy which pervades the
seasons. We feel his style has moved out of its minority and acquired
sensitiveness and precision.

The quality of feeling evident in these poems is related to those about
life in the city. His belief in the dignity and the purposefulness of man
makes him reject the many impositions of modernity as a mass of soul-
sapping irritants. On the whole the city is unfriendly, a conclusion very
likely abetted by the fact that he is an African:

> Nobody knows
> or cares where
> Self comes from
> or goes. My
> knock slams
> the door; reproaches
> fall like soot

> Another self
> dives impenetrably
> inwards trembling.
> Blast of
> autumn leaves
> stuff the conscience
> and ignite.

> Self burns
> totally alone.
> The world is
> singing, teeming
> externally.   (p. 16)

Peters sees this isolation as a fundamental, a *human* rather than a colour problem. His 'wide and resounding reasonableness'[10] shows in the worry over massive pressures generated within the individual and which are unrelieved through a lack of fruitful expression:

> Listen! the agony of the voice
> seeking escape whispers
> Not only the poet's voice
> Philosopher or priest.
> Listen! The average human voice
> in the domed skyscraper
> with every corpuscle in his
> veins worth a dollar or more
> in the bank his face a mask of success.
> Listen to the black cries
> in the tenements.   (p. 60)

The breakdown of traditional means of communication, of self-expression, pushed the individual into isolation. Inevitably the gathering of forces seeks a way out.[11]

The hostility of the city is clear in Poem 11. He sought in this poem a rhythm of ideas – discussed earlier – to assemble a brief, evocative, opening stanza about the nightmarish quality of city life:

> Atmosphere!
> meadows, trees ripe aflame
> cattle netted by highways;
> masked highways fleeing past
> adverts, lights, cables
> Noise, squeaking, breaking
> grinding heaving, swearing whining
> fleeing confusedly into darkness, deep night.   (p. 24)

We submit to the shape, movement, the contrasting light and darkness, to confusion evoked in three dimensions. Our senses are assaulted, over the next two stanzas, wherein Peters talks of the intrusions – mechanical, noisy, and remorseless – which destroy privacy, the 'lights, hallucinations / doorbells like sirens, telephones / answer the telephone / brake quick; lights changing. / The ground is breaking up', stretching the nerves beyond repair. And is not sterility suggested powerfully by the 'underground Tubes masturbating / the earth in draughts'?[12]

More than most African poets writing in English, Peters's work is a criticism of life. And the life he sought to examine is cosmopolitan rather than tribal. There is much he dislikes. This accounts for the carping in his poetry. He is too busy identifying symptoms and illnesses to make anything positive out of it; a real pity, as when he does the results are more than gratifying.

It should be clear from the foregoing that Peters has the resources to write powerful poetry. His imaginative stamina seems capable of rising to most occasions. But none of the poems discussed so far has a consistent forcefulness. It is only in Poem 36 that he succeeds in committing the full stylistic weight, and delicacy, into a poem. The result is exceptional for a combination of penetration and subtlety, of profound matters undertaken with a light yet vivifying touch.

Poem 36 is both a discussion of the positive, creative sensibility of the poet, and a demonstration of its capacity to engage to the utmost the main impulses of his thought. A fortunate conjunction of circumstances enabled the full stylistic powers to reach into the very centres of thinking to offer an excellent example of what the poet can do to educate:

> On a wet September morning
>   When vultures hate themselves
> On the beach, against the flooded moorage
>   Along the rocky shelves
> Where seagulls lay their eggs
>   Half under the cracking waves
> With seaweed under my nails
>   Where the coastline bends
> The sea was not the land's end. (p. 63)

The union of time and place creates an actute state of consciousness, of unusually sharp perceptions within which the separateness of objects is blurred to release a remarkably comprehensive view of things. A process is at work; basic distinctions break down – sea and land are not in opposition.

Peters first states a principle of synthesis which through an imaginative effort enables us to see the continuity of creation. Conventional thinking has to be radically modified before the significance of what he propounds is fully understood:

> The world under the sea
>   The sea under the earth
> The sky in the sea
>   Were elemental changes of a world
> As the true life is death
>   Which is the idea inside us

So distinction ends
The plagued centuries
In a weeping jellyfish
The pebble that will be a crown
The moon reflected in a starfish.   (p. 63)

The text seems reasonably clear: in the beginning was flux; then came separation, which has not ceased. Physical creation evolved till the profusion and variety made us forget its common origin and lose a sense of its continuity. By recognizing how past, present, and future, are linked we are prepared to accept both change and the conception of a common destiny. For despite the constant conversion from one state to another, from one purpose to another, the affinity between all parts of creation is there for us to perceive: 'So distinction ends'. Time, the 'plagued centuries' is manifest in the slow evolution of a jellyfish seeking some higher form; the pebble and the reflection of the moon share the same existence, held in a relationship similar to that of the sea and the worlds below and above it.

Structurally, the poem progresses from general statement to a specific experience. Peters is playing tricks with time; the gift of a moment is expanded and poeticized as 'throwback of vision'. With 'amputated feet / Buried in soft sand', he is already immersed in his new, apparently nightmarish, protean world, tracing the evolution of life itself.[13] The precariousness of the undertaking, his uncertainties and fears, are objectified in the shark's attack.

Peters has omitted from the poem some of the stages through which his thought and language passed. Two passages from other poems provide the missing links. When Peters says:

My amputated feet
Buried in soft sand
Within the blue shadows
Were already prehistoric.   (p. 63)

he means that at that moment the contact with the earth enables him to see how all things partake of a single life. His mind moves into the past to consider the origin of things, a subject taken up in Poem 20 where Peters celebrates, through recall, the sheer sensation of being alive:

Time was
When I was green
fresh as a meadow
glowing with stars

Summer was universal
endless April
youth unrivalled
Summer to the skies

Barefoot in thorn bush
baked sand
forests, the world
was open to me . . . (p. 37)

The thought of the last stanza reappears in Poem 36, but with a difference.
Peters has pushed beyond sensation to the metaphysical, so that the experience is reshaped to fit the dominant theme of Poem 36. And the leap is
supported by the concluding stanza of Poem 20:

These I remember
now life has become a system
Yes, and the deep
deep throbbing of the earth. (p. 38)

The throbbings of the earth offer the clues to this expanded understanding.
The world was open to him then, though it is only in Poem 36 that he
gains access.

But as in all such journeys there is the sharp sensation of being assailed.
Peters exploits the peculiar relevance of the language of dreams, its
vividness and pace, to make the impossible seem less improbable. We
expect the imagination to be stretched, and the expectation increases our
readiness to believe. So what we are given, while surrealistic, remains
plausible:

I tried to leap
Out of a shark's way
Far from the cutting teeth
Thundering like a wave
Aimed at my vitals, not my feet. (p. 64)

This image of a shark slashing has a special significance for Peters. In
Poem 46 he is fascinated by its stream-lined brute life 'cutting the emerald /
sea like firewood'. But while recognizing in it 'An immense danger', he is
impressed by its single-minded rapaciousness. Because it:

stabs centrally
by flashes and shadows
with a clean intention
cast in a single grim desire. (p. 91)

the shark enacts that quick, clean slash to the heart of a matter. It takes time for us to appreciate Peters's logic in the choice because the image, although powerful, encourages stock responses:

> Truth is naked
> to be slashed at cleanly
> shedding ceremonial robes
> of undesirable thoughts
> emotions, words
> complexes. Diving pneumatically
> not with acolytes and candles,
> cleaned sharply to the bone
> like a skilled executioner.   (p. 91)

This is central to Peters's poetry, though here the process of pushing and understanding belongs to an intermediate stage. It is in Poem 36, moved by a compulsion to know of the nature of life, that the full sophistication develops. The conjunction of circumstances is such that he cannot choose but see. Therefore, while he feels rooted and helpless, he is in fact reaching into the sources of primaeval life: his 'vegetable feet' had 'planted roots / Among the symbiozing weeds / Which issued from my feet'. Perception is a form of initiation. What takes place in Poem 36 can be compared in emotional intensity to Gabriel Okara's 'The Snow Flakes Sail Gently Down', and, to a lesser extent, Christopher Okigbo's *Heavensgate*. Okara 'dreamed a dream' and discloses its contents when he comes out of it. Peters's use of the device is more subtle, starting from a specific time and place, then moving into an inner world:

> I could not move;
> I say I could not move
> My vegetable feet;
> But still the tumbling jaws.   (p. 64)

Through this nightmare, he arrives at that point of final despair which is also, paradoxically, the point of illumination:

> Only a silent yell
> Rang through time's corridors
> To the farthest end
> Where the amoeba becomes
> The fire, water and air;
> Where the primaeval fruit still hangs
> So to the other end
> Where planets are but continents
> Deep in the future
> That is darker and older
> Than the past.   (p. 64)

107

Here is time past, time present and time future. It is the equivalent of Krishna's understanding of the *Om* in the Hindu Scriptures. For what Peters claims is a metaphysical possession, an understanding of mortality and change, and, in a sense, to understand is to reach beyond both.

Peters develops his insight through a series of unmistakable correlations. He sees beyond the 'farthest end', relates the amoeba, popularly considered the lowest form of life, to the elemental realities. Very little is urged directly; much is implied; we are made to *feel* the drama. Concurrently, the mind ventures into the future, to the time when technology will make planets as close as continents. To know is to understand. Hence the 'silent yell' that summed up his anguish is converted into an 'echo' which:

> burst inside me
> Like a great harmonic chord
> Violins of love and happy voices
> The pagan trumpet blast
> Swamping the lamentation of the horn
> Then the heraldic drums
> In slow crescendo rising
> Crashed through my senses
> Into a new present
> Which is the future. (p. 65)

The release is carried in the musical notation. Peters wants to convey the benefits accruing from the enlargement of the senses. The music, 'Boundless in all her forms', gives a 'new awareness' and a higher state of feeling of being fed by new insights. It responds powerfully, feels 'vibrations'. Peters seeks, not the unity of being, but the unity of creation. And this, once glimpsed, equips the perceiver with a superior understanding.

The strengths of Poem 36 are substantial. The incisiveness, the superiority traceable in a number of poems, come together with a telling neatness. This is why it is a rare poem. Its simplicities are deceptive in that their total effect is devastating.

Poems such as 'Consider a snail' (29), 'The first rose of the season' (35), 'Sunset climbs in vain' (27) while not as consistently powerful, show a complex mind coming to understand itself by pushing a line of thinking and feeling to the limit. Their main contribution is the clarity of purpose, the point of his poetry. Peters hardly ever loses sight of what he is doing. What I am driving at becomes clearer if we speculate on the possible effects if a similar exercise in self-understanding had been undertaken by Kofi Awoonor. We can hardly imagine Peters, with his purposes, writing in a fashion that is cavalier rather than liberating.

On the whole, Peters's work, is relatively free from fashionable embarrassments. It transcends remarkably the preoccupations of the literary environment constructed for him, and which Kofi Awoonor appears to have found congenial to an extent that the confrontation of the traditional and the Western left little room for the more personal problems of the individual.

That combination of audacity and restraint of time and place, of what constitutes inspiration to capture a moment in all richness, enabled Peters to produce his best poem. Below this achievement are poems which, though they do not have that simultaneous power, nevertheless are valuable for their insights into life and contacts. We can be confident of finding a human centre, the poet's interest in himself and others. Man is clearly the measure of all things, an equation to which the poetic qualities of his work are plainly related. And this is an attitude that could do more for the growth of African poetry in English.

NOTES

1. Page reference locate the quotation in *Satellites*, Heinemann, London, 1967, which includes a majority of the poems in the Mbari volume (1963).
2. Senghor has written vigorously and extensively on *Négritude*. These two quotations furnish an indication of his preoccupations:

> It has often been said that the Negro is the man of Nature. By tradition he lives off the soil and with the soil, in and by the Cosmos. He is sensual, a being with open senses, with no intermediary between subject and object, himself at once the subject and the object. He is, first of all, sounds, scents, rhythms, forms and colours; I would say that he is touch, before being eye like the white European. He feels more than he sees; he feels himself. It is in himself, in his own flesh, that he receives and feels the radiations which emanate from every existing object. Stimulated, he responds to the call, and abandons himself, going from subject to object, from Me to Thee on the vibrations of the Other: he is not assimilated: he assimilates himself with the other, which is the best road to knowledge.

> 'The Spirit of Civilization', *Présence Africaine*, Nos 8, 9, 10 June–November, 1956, p. 52.

> Negritude itself is a myth (I am not using the word in any pejorative sense), but a living, dynamic one, which evolves with its circumstances into a form of humanism.
> 'Negritude and African Socialism,' *African Affairs: 2*, St Anthony's Papers, No. 15, ed. Kenneth Kirkwood, London, Chatto and Windus, 1963, p. 13.

The volume of critical literature on negritude is large. A useful list of articles is available in Barbara Abrash's *Black African Literature since 1952, Works and Criticism,* Johnson Reprint Corporation (New York, 1967). **109**

3. The exchange between Paul Edwards and Nkem Nwanko in *Transition*, Nos. 12 and 15, give some idea of the difficulties involved in the question of critical standards. Among the articles dealing with the question are Clive H. Wake, 'African Literary Criticism', *Comparative Literature Studies*, Vol. I, No. 3 (1964); Edgar Wright, 'African Literature I: Problems of Criticism', *Journal of Commonwealth Literature*, No. 2 (December 1966); John F. Povey, 'Canons of Criticism for Neo-African Literature', *African Proceedings*, III (1966); Donald Stuart, 'African Literature III: The Modern Writer in His Context', *Journal of Commonwealth Literature*, No. 4 (December 1967); Joseph O. O. Okpaku, 'Culture and criticism – African critical standards for African literature and the arts', *Journal of the New African Literature and the Arts* (Spring, 1967).

4. Peters's use of established stanzaic forms has given us some of the most gracious examples to come from Africa. But despite achieving a melli-fluous quality, at their weakest they are exercises in stock sentiment. 'When winter is over' (33) and 'The fire has gone out' (41) are two examples from his Mbari volume which he wisely did not take into *Satellites*. It is significant that they are very 'English' poems.

5. When taken to unusual lengths, the technique can be self-defeating, as in Poem 13 or 33. In the former Peters is so busy putting his subject across that he becomes insensitive to it. The result is an over-insistent, and therefore unbalanced, catalogue:

> Clawed green eyed
> Feline of night
> Palsied breasted
> Selling old boot
> On wet pavement
> In hour-glass baskets.
> Coconut bellied
> Unyielding Copra
> Gland exhausted
> Love fatigued
> Worm tunnelled sod.

It is difficult not to feel revulsion; there is no variation, no abatement in power. While we do not doubt that each statement is substantially true, their total import is overwhelming, to such an extent that Peters's attempt to enlist our sympathy for this poor 'Prostituted fruit of Eve' fails completely. We cannot see how she can be a 'Friend of the falling star' or be a 'victim of the lonely bed . She is more victim than friend, and a victim of something more immense, more corrupt, than a lonely bed. We might go so far as to say that Peters's success with the technique destroys the poem. But when utilized with circumspection, the technique adds considerably to the overall power of a poem.

6. It would be a revealing exercise to compare the way Peters and Dennis Brutus handle nature.

7. E.g.

> Penetration is all
> heavily nagging
> like a mad worm
> to a central unity
> Reality lies beyond
>
> Fantasy and imagination
> soar like a vice
> toward integration
> yellow petals in amalgam.   (p. 26).

8. A number of issues and reflections in *The Second Round* (London, Heinemann Educational Books, 1965) are pertinent to the poetry: 'He [Dr Kawa] mused over the quick substitution of his appetite for the burnt skeletons of the English autumn countryside into his love of the ruthlessness and dynamism of the African bush, and the human pathos which underlay the calm flow of conviviality.' (p. 27).

9. In Poem 3, the 'Sound of the ocean' has its equivalent in the 'tumble in harmonies inside me'. The pastoral elements in Poem 20 re-create the idyllic youth of the poet.

10. Ann Tibble, *African–English Literature* (London, Peter Owen, 1965), p. 93. Dr Kawa's unspoken thoughts are revealing:

> *'I'd like to see you happy and not scared. I'd like to see black men happy because they've got more than the candle inside a magic lantern to be proud of. I want to see all men happy because it's the only way I can be happy, I want to see everything that lives drink in the sunlight and feel safe and warm inside.'*
>
> *The Second Round*, p. 42.

12. Life in the city is twisted. Even the autumnal beauty he cherishes and celebrates with such fervour is not free from the taint of decay, death, or of old women 'probing their coffins' (28). 'Lost Friends' (39), Poems 43, 49, 53, and 54 all attack the insidious influences of city life.

13. See the discussion of the poem by Gerald Moore in 'The Negro Poet and his Landscape', *Introduction to African Literature*, ed. Ulli Beier (Longmans, London, 1967).

Literature and Resistance in South Africa: Two Zulu Poets

Maria K. Mootry

What is the role of an intellectual whose people are an oppressed group struggling for new or renewed nationhood? How can he, from a position inherently disengaged and analytical, involve himself immediately and vitally in that struggle? This question Frantz Fanon answers in his hand-book for black revolution, *The Wretched of the Earth*. Recognizing the spiritual, cultural, and psychological, ravages of the colonizer on the colonized, Fanon places the onus of recovery on the intellectual. To legitimize the people's past; to restore the people's image; to reflect the people's evolution to national consciousness – these are the intellectual's tasks. But, in Fanon's view, he must first undergo a process of evolution himself. This evolution consists of three stages. In the first, the intellectual assimilates the colonizer's culture; in the second, he rejects this culture violently, often embracing negative stereotypes of his people in his effort to rebel; in the last, he frees himself from mere reaction to create a national literature or art based on the dynamic fight for freedom. Within this framework the concept of negritude or 'black is beautiful' becomes an anathema, as much as poetry in imitation of Shakespeare or art after Renoir. The mythologization of the people, based on the oppressor's exaggerations, simply expresses a new form of degradation.[1]

As with all formulae, when applied to actual literary achievements Fanon's categories are inelastic. His assumption is that an intellectual's thought and its expression could not reflect two or three stages of evolution at once. The purpose of this paper is to demonstrate how two Zulu poets fused the elements of the European Romantic tradition with their oral legacy to create poetry of protest and resistance. Benedict Wallet Vilakazi and Herbert Dhlomo, who effected the birth of written Zulu literature in the twentieth century, dominated the entire decade of the thirties. Each had been schooled in English literature and steeped in his oral tradition. Filled with a love of the Zulu people and their heritage, Vilakazi, possibly

because of temperament, carried his art to the level of protest only; while

Dhlomo, as he expresses himself in *Valley of a Thousand Hills*, moved to the level of resistance. The works which will be considered here are Vilakazi's *Zulu Horizons*, which is a compilation and translation into English of his two volumes, *Inkondlo kaZulu* (*Zulu Songs*) and *Amal 'Ezulu* (*Zulu Horizons*); and Dhlomo's *Valley of a Thousand Hills*.* The first section of the paper will present characteristics of both the European and Zulu traditions; the second section will trace elements of each in the poets' works and attempt to relate them to manifestations of political consciousness.

AFRICANS AND ROMANTICS

All critics of Vilakazi and Dhlomo stress their artistic debt to the English Romantic poets – a debt expressed in form and sentiment. D. Mck. Malcolm, in the introduction to *Zulu Horizons*, explains that in studying for his undergraduate degree, Vilakazi 'became aware of the English poets of the Romantic period and was fired with the ambition of doing for Zulu literature what they had done for English'.[2] When the characteristics of the Romantic writers are listed it is clear that their style and thought, in some areas, was peculiarly appropriate for a Zulu poet in the first half of the twentieth century. On an ideological level, the Romantic tradition was characterized by a faith in the imagination and in intuition which was most frequently expressed in the tendency to read meanings into landscapes. Along with this went a strong sense of man's oneness with nature. The poet was regarded as a kind of high-priest. In his uncompromising individualism, he denounced industrial development, all forms of institutions, and all sources of human oppression. He was preoccupied with revolution, often taking a leftist political stance and believing in man's perfectibility; but at the same time he was prone to a powerful sense of disillusionment which reflected his perfectionist standards.

On a formal level, the poet presented himself with a direct appeal to his reader rather than through ironic detachment, often using a dramatic tone. He used images full of nuance and suggestion. In line with his iconoclastic stance, he mixed his styles at will, including the elegiac, the lyrical and the meditative.

The Romantic tradition, then, contained escapist as well as involved proclivities. The clouded view of nature as sympathetic to man and as an automatic source of inspiration and well-being denies the necessary social condition of man. Persistent sombre notes of despair, melancholy, confusion, and unrest, are often signs of a failure to deal with reality. The emphasis on individualism and anti-institutionalism, in one sense, is an

* Dhlomo also wrote fourteen plays, but this paper is limited to the genre of poetry.

escape from the acknowledgment of communal origin and destiny. On the other hand, the aura of revolution emanating from the Romantic tradition was entirely relevant to the needs of the Zulu peoples; seemingly everywhere the downtrodden revolted, championed by the English poet: Greek against Turk, Italian against Austrian, Black against White (San Domingo); and Frenchman against Frenchman. The emphasis was on activism:

> Wordsworth interested himself in the abolition of the slave trade, Coleridge once dreamed of founding a utopian community in the New World, Blake saw existing European churches and governments as the engines of Satan, Shelley and Byron envisioned a new Hellas rising out of the ashes of the Old Greece, and Byron himself, after aiding for some time the Italian underground, died in Greece trying to bring the new Hellas about.[3]

The poets' anti-industrialism paralleled protest against the economic exploitation of black Africans by Englishmen and Afrikaners. And, finally, the view of the poet as 'unacknowledged legislator of the world', is analogous to Fanon's demand that the artist/intellectual assume the role of leader and legitimizer.

The question then arises of the matter of selection and emphasis. Vilakazi explored the Romantic tradition intensely, with positive and negative results. Weighted by Romantic escapist sensibility, sometimes his poetry loses its originality and power altogether. At other times, even though he uses rhyme and addresses a lark or an urn, Vilakazi introduces images and ideas from his Zulu heritage, creating a syncretic work which derives potency from its unique expression. Dhlomo, whose poem is a mixture of many styles, including songs and monologues, makes less complete use of either tradition; or perhaps it should be said that he uses the traditions to his own ends. His poem is therefore a variegated entity that defies classification. Throughout, it operates on several levels of meaning, progressing primarily through complex, ostensibly Romantic, symbolism to its emphatic conclusion.

ZULU HORIZONS

Turning to Vilakazi's poetry, three titles are often pointed out as directly influenced by Keats and Shelley. *Ukhamba luka-Sonkomose* ('Sonkomose's Bowl'), *Inqomfi* ('The Lark') and *We Moya!* (Hail Wind!') are presumably modelled on Keats's 'Ode to a Grecian Urn', and Shelley's 'To a Skylark' and 'Ode to the West Wind', respectively.

The inspiration of 'Sonkomose's Bowl' was an old family pot from which the poet's grandfather had drunk. As the poet gazes at the bowl, memories of the past burst upon his consciousness, creating a sense of communion with his grandfather. This interaction with the object immediately establishes a relationship very different from that of Keats with his urn. The main thrust of Keats's poem is on the artistic distance of the urn. It is a 'cold pastoral' which preaches an abstract truth. Vilakazi's initial apostrophe establishes an atmosphere of warmth and immediacy; a very *human* encounter. In a dramatic tone, he speaks to his ancestor:

> Grandsire, although I did not know you,
> Yet I can commune with you
> And even though I cannot see you,
> This I see: the bending backs
> Of those who say you are their sire,
> And they have given me this insight.

The bowl, no simple *objet d'art*, has been used by the grandfather:

> Here, before me, is a bowl,
> And, from this vessel, once you drank,
> You, son of the Mzwangedwa tribe,
> You who went your ways alone
> And did not ever think to own
> That in its depths were precious secrets.

The poem also incorporates two formal characteristics from the *izibongo*, i.e. the naming of the person addressed or use of epithet ('son of the Mzwangedwa tribe') and the use of repetition plus extension of statement through a consecutive tense:

> You, son of the Mzwangedwa tribe,
> You who went your ways alone
> And did not ever think to own, etc.

The third stanza expresses the happy sense of communion of past, present, and future. In the fourth stanza the use of names derives from the oral tradition in much of Africa. Professor Klaus Wachsmann, in his lectures, has commented on the special emotional potency of names in oral recitations. Vilakazi himself wrote of names that 'stab us like spears: each one is magic'. Thus, the three names in the stanza function in a way unknown to the European written tradition:

> Vessel, in you I see the hills
> Whose name is yours, O Sonkomose,
> Inherited by your son, Mkhwethu,
> Scattered with many herds of cattle,
> Which, by Nkombose my father's daughter,
> Proclaim you 'Encircler of the Hills.'

The fifth stanza includes a direct quotation from a praise epithet:

> I fear not even seers and sages
> Whose lips have touched this bowl,
> Can praise the Mkhwethus in these words:
> 'The ravenous beast whose growl was heard
> That time it stirred and fed at Bulawayo
> Where gorgeous crimson grasses grow.'

Here, interestingly, the poet defies his customs by praising his family on his mother's side (the Mkhwethu) who turned grass crimson with blood as great warriors and founded the Matabele nation in Southern Rhodesia.

The sixth and final stanza reiterates the poet's concept of the bowl and its goblet as retainers of his Zulu heritage. The amber liquid of the goblet reminds him of yet another ancestral figure whom he names, Qwabe, brother of Zulu, founder of the Zulu tribe. The closing lines, addressed to the goblet, beautifully complete the personal veneration of the poet for the bowl and what it symbolizes:

> You are wedded to this vessel
> And everything this vessel holds.

Inqomfi ('The Lark'), written in two parts at different times, is a less successful poem. Since the first six stanzas were composed as a unit and can be considered a complete poem, only these will be discussed. The remaining stanzas are rather superfluous, adding little to either the thought or form. In comparing this poem with Shelley's, a case similar to the above analysis could be made. But here it is less the verbal form that varies than the imagery, detail and sensibility. Shelley's bird is pure spirit ('Bird thou never wert') and as such knows only pure joy. Shelley's theme is his plea that the bird teach him the secret of its music so that the world would be compelled to listen to him. Vilakazi's lark, though it represents spirit, is deliberately linked to the African soil. It leads no idyllic existence, but suffers from the menace of the iguana and the deadly mamba snake, hawks, and poisoned Bushman arrows. It eats tasty locusts, which for Shelley's lark is inconceivable. In the end the bird symbolizes less a remote disembodied spirit than an oracle, a tool of the supernatural forces which govern the destinies of men. The following stanzas are illustrative:

> Oh, you who lay those eggs of dappled colours,
> Hiding them well within the grassy tufts
> Where neither iguana comes nor mamba glides,
> Sing clear above them songs inspiring courage
> And drive away the hawks that would consume them
> During your flights in search of tasty locusts.

What meaning has that rich and fadeless colour,
That splash of glowing crimson on your throat;
Who pierced you with those sharp and fatal arrows,
Known to Bushmen in their rocky caves?
Your symbol this, a flag of flame
To scorch the deaf who spurn your counselling!

If you should fly before a traveller,
The elders say that his affairs will prosper;
But woe to him when you behind
Shall soar across his path, and, like the buzzard,
Sing when the clouds conceal the sun. Ill omen!
You are an oracle, bird, you prophesy!

Of the three poems, *We Moya!* ('Hail Wind!') is closest to the European
tradition. In it Vilakazi shows the same concept of nature as Shelley in his
'Ode to the West Wind'. To Shelley, the rough wind is a destroyer and
preserver, to which he prays for artistic rebirth:

> Scatter, as from an unextinguish'd hearth
> Ashes and sparks, my words among mankind!
> Be through my lips to unawaken'd earth
>
> The trumpet of a prophecy![4]

Like Shelley, Vilakazi apostrophizes the wind, ending with a plea for a
union with it that will revive the poet.[5] Returning to Fanon's categories,
this poem falls easily into assimilationist literature or what Jahnheinz Jahn
termed 'apprentice literature'. Its pervasive melancholy is trite; its
imitative language lacks the strength of original imagery. Only two stanzas
attain any power of expression, and these contain details derived from the
poet's background. By way of illustration, the two stanzas labelled *a* and *b*
can be compared with those that follow:

> (*a*) Come soon, the sun has risen
> And pleasant is the hill
> Where you in strength can rival
> The houses of the Ngangas.
>
> Come let us both be merry
> And feel that strong desire
> That's born of restlessness
> Whose enemy is sloth.
>
> (*b*) And you foretell the rain,
> (Wafting the scent of melons
> That ripen with the pumpkins)
> For mealie plants and berries.

Come, wind! O come and lighten
My heart that feels so heavy
And let me die when you die.

Elements from the *izibongo* found in Vilakazi's first volume and used
even more extensively in the second are: the use of names and praise-
names; the use of metaphors, similes and imagery from Zulu plant and
animal life; the use of a dramatic tone; the use of a confident epic tone;
the use of parallel structures; and the use of repetition. In the interest of
time and space, four poems from *Inkondlo kaZulu* (the first volume in
Zulu Horizons) will be used to illustrate the prevalence of these techniques.
They are (*a*) *Inkelekele yakwaXhoza* ('The Xhosa Calamity'); (*b*) *Khalani
maZulu* ('Weep, You Zulus!'); (*c*) *UShaka kaSenzangakhona* ('Shaka, Son
of Senzangakhona') and (*d*) *Phezu kwethuna likaShaka* ('Over the Grave of
Shaka'). Here are the examples.

A. Use of names:

> (*a*) Ah! speak and tell me, where are *Tshiwo*
> And other chiefs, men like *Hanahana*
> *Xiniha, Menziwa,* and *Hahabe,*
> *Manxa, Nukwa* and *Nqabisile?*
> Where do they sleep, the maids of *Xhosa,*
> *Sutho, Joli, Nomalizo?*
> Speak and tell me, where are *Hintsa,*
> The *Xhosa* chiefs, the *Xhosa* women –
> Adorned with feathers, vulture, ostrich –
> Who danced at *Qonce* and at *Monti?* (p. 23)

(Note the cumulative effect of a catalogue of names.)

> (*b*) The great bird has died, and there rotted
> The bones of the children of *Qwabe.*
> And then came a man, *Dinuzulu,*
> Who lived at the place, *Sikhwebezi,*
> The home of the leading *uSuthu;*
> A new one at *emaHhashini*
> He built on a hill near *Nongoma.* (p. 40)

(Note powerful effect of having names at end of each line.)

> (*c*) You, *Shaka,* were the very image
> Of sages whom we know today,
> Fighting all the would-be traitors.
> Many opposed you, all were hurled
> Upon the assegais and clubs.
> *Zwide* fell; he fell because
> He sought to elevate himself

Above you. Broken and crushed he fell
And all his followers disputed:
They, like *Matiwane* quarrelled.   (p. 58)

(Note the structuring function of the names.)

(*d*) Come to your children again, O *Zulu*!
Greatest of all the *uSuthu* Chiefs,
So that the world may see once more,
O fearless son of *Menzi*,
The power of your famous forbears,
The fame the *Qulusis* still retain.   (p. 74)

(Again, note the structuring function of the names.)

B. Use of Praise-names:

(*a*) The great bird has died . . .   (p. 40)

To the mountain that shelters the Lion
From the fear of the thundering heavens.   (p. 41)

And some saw Monase
Who gazed at Mahhashini
And wept like the abaQulusi. . . .   (p. 42)

(Note extension through a grammatical unit dependent upon the
statement and through a consecutive tense.)

(*b*) . . . . the mighty Cub
Of Phunga and of Xaba who was borne
Upon the shoulders of the sun,
Cared for and nurtured by the moon,
For he was destined to discover trails
Of Zulus bound for Pondoland.   (p. 57)

(Note statement, extension, development, and conclusion.)

(*c*) Your tombstone has displaced them, Shaka,
Mountain whose spirit is a lion
Sheltering from the storms of heaven!
You who drank from clear deep pools,
As though a honeysucker, also
Drank from shallow muddy water
That soils the tufted bending head
And stains the tips of trailing wings.   (p.77)

(Note lyricism and imagery of harmless, delicate, animal, which
is also characteristic of pre-Shakan praise-poem.)   **119**

C. Metaphors, similes and imagery from Zulu plant and animal life:

> (See above examples which contain references to bird, hill, mountain, lion, cub, sun, moon, pool, and honeysucker)

D. Use of dramatic address:

> (*a*) Battalions of Zulus, awaken!
> Gather your weapons and listen!
> Awaken, uSuthu detachments!
> And yours Mandlakazi, awake!
> What manner of sleep has benumbed you?
> Can you not hear that the Zulus
> Are seething as though they were maggots? (p. 38)

> (*b*) Listen to me, you simpletons,
> You who hear me speak
> Until I waste to thinness of a rake ... (p. 57)

> Listen to me, you useless men! (p. 57)

> You, Shaka, were the very image
> Of sages whom we know today ... (p. 58)

> (Shaka is addressed throughout.)

> (*c*) Come to your children again, O Zulu!
> Greatest of all the uSuthu chiefs ... (p. 74)

> Ring out the bells,
> You Zulu chiefs ... (p. 75)

> Rise from beneath that tomb, O shaka (p. 78)

E. Use of a Confident Epic-like tone:

(See examples of direct address).

The confident tone derives primarily from contemplation of past; examples are numerous but this stanza offers a typical rendering:

> (*d*) And one who fled was grey-heaired Nxaba;
> He scaled the great uBombo mountains.
> But in the land of the Basutos
> Mshweshe was a scourge: he plundered!
> He lured them into uBusiko,

> Establishing new rules and customs
> For the baKgatla and the Pedi,
> Giving no ground and spreading Northward.
> Time passed and all the nations feared him;
> Great were his gains and he a marvel. (p. 61)

(This is the intellectual exalting and legitimizing his past; his attitude might be contrasted to Mofolo's moralizing against Shaka in his historical novel, *Chaka*. Jahn rightfully called this type of poetry 'indirect protest.'[6]

F. Use of parallel structures and repetition:

(*a*) 'Oh you who would hinder the Zulus,
    Oh you who would conquer their kingdom,
    All, all will be slaughtered and perish.' (p. 40)

(*b*) Later inherited by Shaka:
    He who devoured the rich and poor,
    He who destroyed the forests, herds and rushes. (p. 57)

    He dwelt among the Portuguese
    Where still his people could survive,
    Free from the terrors of the night,
    Free from the marching of the troops,
    Free from the clashing of the shields. (p. 61)

(*c*) Those stones at Nkandla cover him,
    Him, not helped across the river,
    Him his people doomed through envy,
    Him they branded as a tyrant. (p. 75)

Interestingly, while Zulu critics such as D. D. T. Jabavu and C. L. S. Nyembezi admit that Vilakazi made some use of the oral tradition, especially in his second volume of poetry, they emphasize the European influence on the poet. It is partially in reaction to their assessment that the above analysis has attempted to show that, even where Vilakazi used European rhyme and stanza form, i.e. in his first volume of poetry, elements from the *izibongo* were a substantial part of the verse. Jabavu describes this volume as an example of 'English influence *in excelsis*'; this he attributed to 'its outright imitation of English modes (metres long, short, and common; all varieties of stanzas, elegiacs, sonnets, rhymes and even the heroic couplet reminiscent of Pope and Dryden) all punctiliously observed'.[7] Nyembezi emphasized Vilakazi's 'Europeanness' when he observed,

And yet among the Zulus Vilakazi is remembered more as a poet than as a prose-writer; he was mainly responsible for developing poetry whose form departed radically from the traditional *izibongo* (or praises). He experimented with European forms. He divided his poems into regular stanzas. He also experimented with rhyme.[8] **121**

Unfortunately, Vilakazi's poetic theory probably contributed to his critics' judgements. In 'The Conception and Development of Poetry in Zulu', he called for faithful imitation of the colonizer's form. 'Educated poets,' he felt, had to study the standards of Classical or European poetry; these standards would help to arouse 'finer and deeper feelings' because of the impact of the 'outer world' on their sensitive souls. He added emphatically:

> I do not believe in form; I rely more on the spirit of poetry. Form tends to reduce everything to mechanical standards and mathematical formulae. But we have to use some form to embody or clothe the beautiful spirit of our poetry. We have no definite form so far, and our starting point will be at the standards given us by the Western education we have imbibed at college. We are beginning the work which may be given perfect form in generations to come. I believe, therefore, it is absolutely necessary that, in composing some poems, we ought to rhyme and decorate our poetic images with definite stanza forms.[9]

What conclusions can be drawn from Vilakazi's use of historical themes and techniques from the oral tradition relative to the question of political consciousness? One thing is clear. The use of historical themes or praise-poem structure does not automatically indicate escapism, nor does it automatically create protest or a militant stance. In other words, varied uses can be made of an oral tradition. Looking into the past can create a sense of regret and immobility, as when Vilakazi addressed Shaka in disillusionment, crying 'Would that our times were yours, O Shaka!'[10] The structure of the praise-poem can be used to flatter the colonizer (almost all missionaries and other whites have had praise-poems made for them), or to deride him (the oft-quoted mock-praise by Mqhayi is a famous example[11]). In the latter case, the form achieves a level of satirical protest, or better yet, protest-through-satire. One fascinating example of this use of the praise-poem appeared in the Xhosa journal, *Isigidimi* (1871). It was written by UHadi Waseluhlangeni ('The Harp of the Nation'), whom A. C. Jordan described as a writer of great intellectual integrity, widely read by literate Black South Africans. 'Hadi' protested against the journal's support of whites and bias against its own people and suggested that this poem be a model for other poets:

Arise, ye sons of the Mountain-at-Night!
The hyena howls, the white hyena,
All ravenous for the bones of Moshoeshoe,
Of Moshoeshoe who sleeps high up on the mountain.

Its belly hangs heavy and drags on the ground,
All gorged with the bones of warrior-kings;
Its mouth is red with the blood of Sandile.

Awake, rock-rabbits of the Mountain-at-Night!
She darts out her tongue to the very skies,
That rabbit-snake with female breasts
Who sucked and fostered the trusting Fingos,
Thereafter to eat them alive.[12]

Except that Sandile is a Xhosa chief and the rabbit-snake represents Queen Victoria, not much commentary is needed here.

But to return to Vilakazi: it seems that he used his Zulu heritage largely on an artistic basis and with the purpose of recapturing the past. As indicated earlier, this might have been due to his temperament, which seems to have been melancholy and resigned. His most famous and overt protest poem, 'In the Gold Mines', significantly is neither in the Romantic nor the praise-poem tradition, but in simple dramatic stanzas. Equally significant, however, is the poet's use of the allegorical mode characteristic of his oral tradition. As in UHadi's poem quoted above, black men are represented as rock-rabbits, but these rock-rabbits have been turned into moles who burrow deep into the earth. The machines are brothers of the black men but they are luckier: they face no prospect of lung disease. Even here Vilakazi's overall tone is plaintive; he feels confused, dispirited. Once this plaintive note rises to defiance, when the poet is bolstered by thoughts of his past:

> Take care! Though now our arms are weak,
> Once their power made dark the skies,
> And earth was torn and nations reeled,
> The Great White Queen lost many sons,
> Paul Kruger's children too we slaughtered.
> Then we, the conquerors, were defeated.
> And now I dream, Oh thing of Iron!
> Dream that this land – my fathers' land –
> Shall be my fathers' sons' again.   (p. 173)

But then Vilakazi slips back into his plaintive mode, calling on his fathers to end his wretchedness. After receiving no answer, he concludes his poem with a startling, chilling, plea for withdrawal into death.

VALLEY OF A THOUSAND HILLS

Unlike any of Vilakazi's protest poems, Dhlomo's *Valley of a Thousana Hills* climaxes in an overt, impassioned cry for the Zulu people to rise, revolt and establish their hegemony of African civilization. But Dhlomo's achievement, like Vilakazi's, seems to have been misinterpreted by his critics. Writing in *The African Image*, Ezekiel Mphahlele credits Dhlomo with some of the most vigorous protest writing of the twenties and thirties, **123** but his assessment does not do justice to the poet's revolutionary temper. Mphahlele thinks that Dhlomo presents the African primarily as an underdog:

> Throughout the poem runs the wailing of black people who were once proud and majestic but now lie in the dust, but whose conscience is still alive. The poem is Dhlomo's struggle to understand himself, an underdog, the meaning of pain, the problem of power and greed, and also a struggle to invoke his ancestral spirits whose presence he feels in the Valley. . . . His protest imagery is drawn from Byron and Shelley, and his nostalgic melancholy from Keats.[13]

Mphahlele's conclusion is that the Valley remains at once a symbol of despair and hope for the underdog, and that Dhlomo is a hopeless romanticist who prays for a world without pain 'in a scheme of things where life is always pain'.[14]

Mphahlele wrote under the exigency of proving a point when he made his judgement on Dhlomo. Annoyed with the attempts of African intellectuals like Senghor to create the cult of the African personality, Mphahlele denies any such entity, asserting that African character involves a number of qualities ranging from Christian submissiveness to violent intransigence to romanticism. Under these circumstances he missed, either purposefully or through an oversight, the decidedly un-romantic* message of Dhlomo's poem, on a structural and thematic level.

Dhlomo opens his poem with a prologue filled with praise-poem elements but set in a framework of English language, stanzas and rhyme. As an invocation, the prologue contains a catalogue of names and praise-names, and proceeds through dramatic apostrophe and an epic tone. But Dhlomo immediately establishes a mood of urgency, a sense of mission and personal involvement, which overshadows any simplistic historical perspective and anticipates the militant call to action made later in the poem. The first and last stanzas of the prologue establish this mood:

> Mfolozi Black and Mahlabathini!
> Inkandhla, Nongoma and Ulundi!
> Mfolozi White and Umkhambathini!
> . . .
> These men and places call to me!
> They speak out of Eternity!
> I see, I feel, I live it all!
> I rise! and yield before the call!

In the same hyperbolic style, Dhlomo begins the poem proper with lavish praise for the South African landscape. These praises are followed by an

* Romantic in the sense of escapist.

inventory of Zulu gods and warriors in the Homeric tradition. But Dhlomo, a truly versatile poet, intersperses songs with his verse; songs addressed to great Zulu chiefs of the past, praising them and imploring them to save the people. A sense of imminent action is dominant.

Following more praises of the 'heaven-sculptured land', Dhlomo slips into his critique of the oppressor:

> Our human arts in chains of fungus soil
> Of crippling laws and forms have now become
> Commercial pantomime, a reaping field
> For swollen pundits . . .[15]

Dhlomo next proceeds into a negritudinist celebration of the land and its ebonied people ('the whisperings and pangs of love / from black ebonied buoyant hearts'). He then apostrophizes a bird in full Romantic style, contrasting its ability to mould pain, beauty, love and joy into a 'bloom of song', with the desolation of man's existence. But Dhlomo speaks not simply of man, but of the Black man's soul. Portions which indicate this intent are italicised in the following excerpt:

> But here on earth Man's Soul remains the toy
> Of inharmonious processes which long
> Have raged; here where our youth and joys are mocked
> By want and tears; where, like the dead, foul dust
> Shuts tight our door; where age, deemed wise, is rocked
> By scourge and fear and hate! *here where we must*
> *Deceive and fawn, serve shams and crawl like worms a place*
> *To find,* and die to live! where crafty eyes
> Of gain and power, devour devoid of grace! (pp. 11–12)

Next Dhlomo uses an allegory to express his intellectual captivity to his white oppressor and his desire to be free. Europe appears as a succubus, a 'foreign devil beast' to whom the poet gave himself before he realized the beauty of his homeland. Africa is an arum lily which he would now like to gather but cannot, being enthralled by 'ties which strangle'. During the secret night the lily has wafted its scent on a passer-by (the European commercial man), who plucked it and left the poet 'the wilting stem' (pp. 12–14).

Dhlomo's poem progresses through a series of themes. The dominant ones are those of pain and loss, supported by images of serpents and beasts, juxtaposed with the themes of light and hope, supported by images of the dawn and the symbol of the bird.

In section three of the poem, Dhlomo laments the pain of seeing his mother, once wild and free, now serving 'in tears and toil'. Desiring to see **125**

her decked with flowers and smiling, Dhlomo romanticizes the woman she
once was, employing the language of negritude:

> These tasselled miracles of Thousand Land,
> Gift of black gods, experimenting, wise;
> Met, coalesced and found expression in
> Your lovely face, sweet form, deep measured mind,
> Spiritual purity! (pp. 15–16)

He hints that his own restlessness is due to his spiritual inheritance from
his mother (Mother Africa?). Her pure soul, love of the best, and fiery
independent spirit have infused him with a will to fight. For shames that
he suffers daily he vows, 'I of this world, men of this world, oppose. /
Betray and fight!' (p. 16).

Part four finds a continuation of the beast-satanic theme: from the white
female foreign beast the poet shifts to the deriding voice of the devil (the
white man) who seeks to crush the poet's spirit. Here he dramatizes the
colonizer in the act of destroying the colonized's self-concept. After
mocking the poet and calling him a thing 'disgraced, diseased, and powerless', the white man boasts that he has replaced the ancestral gods. The
white man himself is now God, the deity of power and gain. Destruction
impending at the hands of this devil drives the poet to despair. Using
serpent imagery he graphically describes his state:

> Fogs of despondence wrap me round
> In python-like death coils!
> And fling me to the ground
> Despised! a dog full of boils! (p. 19)

It is in this low state that he craves peace, a peace exempt from foul
disease, the peace of death. But in classic Romantic language, a voice from
the hills urges him to look to their beauty and be restored. The poet,
through solitude and introspection, arrives at the truth of Romantic
individualism, declaring the sovereignty of the single Soul ('Thus I am
God! and God is I . . . this Self!').[16]

Had Dhlomo ended with this revelation, Mphahlele's assessment would
have been more than valid. But what is crucial is the poet's direction after
this moment of truth. Through the vehicles of dramatic voices from the
past Dhlomo unfolds his final vision, one which negates all preceding
images of weakness and impotence.

An initial chorus offers the poet consolation, invoking the 'twin shields
of Hope and Light'. With this inspiration, the poet entertains a series of
visions. The first vision is that of the intellectual fulfilling his role as
126 leader and spiritual sustainer of his people. Through his own volition he

toils and sweats 'in song'. He is the miner who works without an overseer, who seeks what is more precious than gold. He sets a tree to feed the un-born; a tree which will sprout the 'evergreen / Rich groves of our Race Soul' (p. 26). Next comes a vision of the true republic. The poet delineates the Tribal Village State in which no commerce destroys the souls of men, no penal institutions make a mockery of justice, and no caste system relegates men to a sub-human status. Dhlomo indulges in a Rousseauistic vision of natural freedom, but his emphasis is on the building of a great Black nation by

> ... lordly men like rock hewn strong,
> Not bent nor burdened with small things
> Of avarice, but bred and taught
> To wrestle with immensities
> And lasting things of nation-wide
> Philosophies of racial growth ... (pp. 28–9)

At this point, voices of the past arise, expressing the sources of con-tentment for each peer group. But this theme of happiness shades into a theme of regeneration:

> Our race feels young!
> Great and far-flung
> Our Rule will be
> When we rise free
> From 'prentice long
> To sing our Song
> Of manhood strong!
> We shall right Wrong,
> And rule proud king,
> Not wretched things! (p. 32)

From this note of hope Dhlomo shifts to the grim present, representing clashes between black and white in the hellish image of encoiled snakes. The black man is now a Christ-like figure, nailed to the 'Cross of Truth Divine' by 'beasts of his own form' (p. 36). Then Dhlomo hears a wail which goads the black nation to 'dig the Past', and learn that the native Soul is not dead, not tamed, not lost, but 'forever blooming out into new beauties deep and fresh ...' (p. 36). This voice appeals to the memory of 'swarthy giant men', who fought unyieldingly against foreign domination.

Another voice, not satisfied with the glorious past, launches into bitter protest against the usurper and ends on a note of resistance and revolt:

> This beauty's not my own! My home is not
> My home! I am an outcast in my land!
> They call me happy while I lie and rot

127

Beneath a foreign yoke in my dear strand!
Midst these sweet hills and dales, under these stars,
To live and to be free, my fathers fought.
Must I still fight and bear anew the scars?
Must freedom e'er with blood, not sweat, be bought?
You ask me whence these yearning words and wild;
You laugh and chide and think you know me well;
I am your patient slave, your harmless child,
You say . . . so tyrants dreamt as ev'n they fell!
My country's not my own, – so will I fight!
My mind is made: I will yet strike for Right.   (pp. 37–8)

A third voice, impatient with the colonizer's aesthetic language, speaks 'in screech of parlance modern'. Sounding the most militant call to arms, this voice completes a cycle: from visions of a past utopia the poet traversed to images of consolation, to exclamations of protest, to cries of resistance, to the call for revolt. In the process he has shifted his form to suit his function. From Romantic effusiveness he shifts to blunt brief couplets paralleling his shift from the theme of personal suffering and confusion to decisive communal action. Dhlomo 'bellows' to his people:

'. . . Arise and fight
For your birthright
Snatched by hands of all clime!
Now is the time
To stir, to shout, to do . . .
To build anew!
We cannot stand and wait:
The hour of Fate
Has come!
. . .
At last the native Soul
Will win the goal.
There is no power can stand
This living band!'   (pp. 39–40)

In the last section, Dhlomo returns to the image of the bird and the symbol of light (the dawn). But now the bird represents the soul of the black nation ('It is our Soul! It lives! It mocks! It sings! It soars! 'Tis great!') and it flies over a new earth ('All earth is purged, and we enthroned!') (p. 41). The dawn, like the dawn in Keita Fodeba's poem,[17] is now the dawn of Revolution.

In conclusion, Dhlomo, like Vilakazi, makes use of both the European and the Zulu oral traditions. Though he certainly makes greater use of the former, he subordinates both to his own ends. His poetry moves on several levels so that the European imagery itself becomes revolutionary. Because of the limited focus of this paper, certain broader questions cannot be

128

taken into consideration. Two relevant ones are: How did the more liberal Smuts régime affect the African intellectual? and What was the nature of Vilakazi's and Dhlomo's audience? The assumption here is that Dhlomo's audience (particularly for *Valley of a Thousand Hills*) consisted of fellow black intellectuals, likewise schooled in the European tradition, who would understand his artistic achievement but have their political souls touched by his fervour. If this is so, then Dhlomo fulfils the first duty of the intellectual,* i.e. to offer an invitation to thought, to de-mystification and to battle. Perhaps the poet already knew what Fanon later cautioned:

It is not enough to try to get back to the people in that past out of which they have already emerged; rather we must join them in that fluctuating movement which they are giving a shape to, and which, as soon as it has started, will be the signal for everything to be called into question.[18]

NOTES

1. Frantz Fanon, *The Wretched of the Earth* (New York, 1968), pp. 210–27. The entire chapter, 'On National Culture,' is relevant.
2. Benedict Wallet Vilakazi, *Zulu Horizons* (Cape Town, 1962), p. 2.
3. William Frost, ed., Romantic and Victorian Poetry (New York, 1950), p. 11.
4. Frost, p. 206.
5. Vilakazi, p. 27.
6. Jahnheinz Jahn, *Neo-African Literature* (New York, 1968). p. 90.
7. D. D. T. Jabavu, *The Influence of English on Bantu Literature* (Lovedale, 1948), p. 11.
8. C. L. S. Nyembezi, *A Review of Zulu Literature* (Pietermaritzburg, 1961), p. 7.
9. B. W. Vilakazi, 'The Conception and Development of Poetry in Zulu', *Bantu Studies*, XII (1938), p. 129.
10. Vilakazi, *Zulu Horizons*, p. 76.
11. Ezekiel Mphahlele, *The African Image* (New York, 1962), p. 168.
12. A. C. Jordan, 'Towards An African Literature', *Africa South*, p. 112.
13. Mphahlele, p. 183.
14. Mphahlele, p. 186.
15. H. I. E. Dhlomo, *Valley of a Thousand Hills* (Durban, 1941), p. 9.
16. Dhlomo, p. 23.
17. Fanon, pp. 227–31.
18. Fanon, p. 227.

* In an oppressed state.

Can the Prisoner Make a Poet?
A Critical Discussion of
Letters to Martha
by Dennis Brutus

Bahadur Tejani

It seems to me to be right to ask several fundamental questions in relation to what Dennis Brutus has to say in this collection and regarding the nature of the publication by Heinemann Educational Books, with reference to the South African situation and its international implications.

To the mind of the East African the white South African is a bizarre inhuman phenomenon. 'Giving arms to South Africa is arming a murderer' Nyerere said to Heath and the world press on 13 October 1970, '. . . the nearest thing to the Jew–German problem under Hitler.'[1] Quite understandably, not until the deeper shades of suspicion have been removed by long personal contact can we believe in anything that is said by a white South African, or view anyone who toes the line of non-resistance without natural hostility.

South Africa's international position and our impressions of that part of the world will and do interact in our reading of these poems. The jacket blurb introduces the book thus: '*Letters to Martha* are poems chiefly of experiences as a political prisoner on Robben Island off Cape Town. On release from prison Dennis Brutus was served with banning orders which made it criminal to write anything, including poetry, which might be published. So these poems were written as "letters" to his sister-in-law, Martha, after his brother had been sent to Robben Island.'[2]

Considering the tone and form of which much more will be said later, we are perforce made to ask 'Were the poems composed *in* or *out* of **130** prison?' How did Brutus or the publishers outwit the South African

Government which made it criminal to write *anything* publishable. Were the poems smuggled out of the country before they saw the light of day there? Or are 'letters' a strategy of form to outwit the Minister of Justice and his censor henchmen? If so when and where were they first published? In October 1962, Brutus had ? urgent message for the world in his first collection of poems published by Mbari. 'Time may be running out at this end: house arrest looms, and it is never sure how much rope(!) one has. It may be more difficult for me to keep in touch in future.'[3]

Given such a setting and such an emergency situation, one feels the publishers ought to have carried the problems of the poet on their shoulders. In a special collection like this, the audience is of crucial importance and the time and specially the circumstances under which Brutus wrote would colour our judgement; would inform our assessment of future products from South African 'revolutionaries'. More than a dozen English poets and half a dozen Afrikaner poets are now exiled from South Africa all over the Western world, while three Afrikaner poets have committed suicide. The world outside certainly needs to know more about the South African literary scene, the poet's condition of existence, what happens to him, and how and under what circumstances.

In the light of this, I see no reason why important political information has been withheld or omitted, when both the publishers and the poet have tried to be as realistic as possible in their presentation, with titles like 'For Daantjee – on a New Coin envelope' while the note at the end of the poem reads, 'While under house arrest' (p. 30). If the reader's mood is to be so far influenced as to be told in the title 'For Canon L. John Collins 5th August 1966 (11.38). En route from London to New York El Al Airlines' (p. 34), or again, '5th August 1966. In flight over the Atlantic after leaving South Africa' (p. 35), then it is reasonable to charge the publishers either with insufficient research on the poet's biographical background, or decided lack of care, or just ignorance of what both the poet and publisher are about. A trick to lull our judgement can be felt in the actual information recorded by the publishers. Can anyone who has known the modern inter-actions between the South African Government and the Africans, and the power of gold and anti-communism with which South Africa baits the great powers, fail to sympathize with this summary of Brutus's career? Singularly responsible for South Africa's Olympic expulsion, arrested in 1963, escaped, handed over to the South African Security Police by the Portuguese, shot in the back while trying again to escape, a teacher for fourteen years, married with eight children, brother in prison, poems written for sister-in-law for her 'grief loss and care' in the poet's own words; the situation is classic. We are justified in turning to the verse with heightened expectation of another Doctor Zhivago confronting us with **131** the destiny of Man under totalitarianism and more, racialism. The response to the poetry when it comes, however, is quite different.

Internal contradictions within the volume present a greater psychological block than expected. Apart from the titles of the poems quoted earlier, which of course do not justify the dramatic title of the collection, *Other Poems from a South African Prison*, what is to be made of the hotch-potch of chronology that the publishers have provided? The opening poem dates back to 1960. It also incidentally sets the tone for the reader's understanding of Brutus, since he is at best with *himself*. 'Absence and hunger mushroom my hemispheres,' he says.

The eighteen poems of the next group are dated 20 December 1965 as *Letters to Martha*, followed by six postscripts to the letters, the sixth one remarkably similar to the sixth letter to Martha, both dealing with refuge into insanity sought by prisoners, a suspicious coincidence. The quite meaningless intrusion of a date at the end of the postscripts in *A Letter to Basil* is backed by equally irritating details of notes on the poems dealing with Blood River Day. Here if anywhere it would have been useful to explain the significance of this day in the South African calendar. These details, of course, break up the main Martha sequence which as we noted is dated 20 December 1965. A page later, no date when it is most needed, but instead simply, 'While under house arrest.' Then on to 2 and 3 July and 5 August 1966, whilst leaving South Africa; though here again a quite elementary mistake is committed by putting the London–New York poem before the South Africa–London poem.

Afterwards the chronology goes haywire. From May and July 1962 we jump to poems on the prison island, though we are not told if it is Robben Island or not. This is followed by titles like 'On the Road' (to or from prison?) and 'Beach' which are really very diverse by comparison to the rest of the work. From here we are shifted to July 1966, April 1962 and then somersaulted into the mid-fifties on p. 45; again to July 1966, 1960 to Colesberg [*sic*]; then to the poem which ought to have taken the opening of the collection as Brutus's Olympic victory over the South African Sports Colour Bar, dated 2 July 1966. Finally titles I and II [*sic*] indicating separate themes dated March 1966.

No continuity of moods, places, situations, or time, can be felt in such an arrangement. The publishers having gone all the way with Brutus's wavering mind have created a waywardness for themselves which is rare. It allows the reader to interpret the poems in any way he likes, despite the carefully contrived façade of places, towns, and dates.

The connecting link between this collection and his Mbari publication *Sirens Knuckles Boots* may therefore be taken as a starting point to discuss **132** the worthiness of his verse. On p. 42 of *Letters to Martha* on 8 July 1966, twenty-two days before he is to leave South Africa, Brutus records his reaction to the harmony of Nature he feels around him (the companionship of nature – trees and winter sun):

> Condemns me once again
> labels me poet dreamer troubador
> unreal unworldly muddle-headed fool
> while the trees nod and swagger.[5]

The operative word is of course 'troubador' to be found here and in the opening poem of *Sirens Knuckles Boots*:

> A troubador, I traverse all my land
> exploring all her wide-flung parts with zest.

The troubador was a figure common in Southern France, Eastern Spain and Northern Italy, singing chiefly of gallantry and chivalry! Commenting on this, Paul Theroux, who assessed Brutus's first collection in *Black Orpheus* said that despite the poet's description of himself as a 'troubador', his verse is very different. To quote, 'Brutus speaking for the millions of black South Africans has been frustrated and turned away and confined and shot at and still nothing has changed. And so he continues to rage.'[6] This may be true, though whether Brutus speaks for the black Africans is a further point to be taken up. Theroux's weightage in favour of the poet is rather personal. He is one of the rare individuals definite about the white man's burden and discusses the subject openly. His articles on the whites in East Africa in *Transition* No. 32, 'Tarzan the Expatriate', created a furore in European circles which we East Africans thought had been forgotten. Theroux's analysis of their motives for coming to East Africa or staying on, touched the mainspring of their psychology and motivation: Capital.

None the less Theroux himself has noted the dichotomy between Brutus's intention and execution, and dismisses the former in favour of the latter. Yet, since the work and the mood occur for a second time, at the very moment when Brutus is leaving South Africa, we must pay serious attention to his intentions. The reoccurrence of the archaic description of himself, far more relevant in the sunny non-racial climate of the Mediterranean, and the mood of the poem, show that the poet listens to the outside voices with a decisiveness which is his weakness. He is struggling to gain self-realization but is far from achieving it. Who is it that labels him with these adjectives, makes him feel unreal and a fool? His social conscience? his family? his friends? or the total situation in South Africa? If it is the last, then, as Lewis Nkosi once said in his essay on South African fiction, **133**

'It might be more prudent to renounce literature temporarily and solve the political problem first.'[7] In the quoted lines there is a frankness which is appreciable since the poet relies heavily on the reader's trust; but his self-assessment shows a lightness of tone and approach towards the function of poetry which is self-condemning.

Here it is fruitful to dwell on the feelings of another who like Brutus fought for freedom at the international level: Dag Hammerskjöld. Both men love justice and peace and use verse for self-expression. But the resolve of Hammerskjöld is different. The timbre of his voice is alive and struggling:

> Weep
> if you can,
> Weep
> But do not complain.
> The way chose you –
> And you must be thankful.[8]

The subjection of the ego to the cause for which he fights is seen in the continuous and terrifying interaction of Hammerskjöld's poetry. His condition of mind furthers the energy he fights with, which in turn furthers the reader's awareness of his cause, his condition, his social life. As against this, we may set the following from the sixteenth poem to Martha. Brutus is told:

> Mister
> This is prison
> just get used to the idea.[9]

And the poet does, with a finality which is frightful. For him no reserves of energy, no courage of beliefs from deep within, no conflict, no fortitude to buoy him against the hostile environment.

Unfortunately for Brutus he is not the only one who has been to prison for his beliefs. 'The European continent has already reached a stage where a man could be told without irony that he should be thankful to be shot and not strangled, decapitated or beaten to death.'[10] Thus wrote Koestler in *The Scum of the Earth* of his prison experience during the German invasion of France in 1939–40. Such a starkly naked understanding of the condition of Man and himself, makes the writer utterly realistic and therefore fully aware of what is happening around him. Prison life is 'An undramatic everyday torture which transformed our crowd within a few weeks into grey-faced, hollow-eyed, apathetic wrecks'.[11] The prisoners had to carry sixty pounds of human excreta between two men pushing the

134 bins on to trucks in freezing cold, empty them into the river and scrub the

bins clean in icy water, breaking the ice if necessary. Koestler adds, 'But the Latrine Squad had only to work one hour in the morning, one in the afternoon, while the navvies, stone-breakers and road builders had to work six. In my present occupation it was quit for two hours of nausea a day and for this very reason the Latrine Squad was the most coveted form of work in the camp. This filthiest and most degrading labour was a desirable escape from the murderous strain and monotony of the others'.[12]

Most of the inmates, including Koestler, were, like Brutus, political prisoners – the European left-wing socialists, White-Russians, communists, and so forth. Koestler's style allows us the freedom to see for ourselves. As can be seen above, there is a firmness in approach, both to the life of the prison and to experience in general, which makes the reader aware with a striking clarity of the normalcy of his own world and the abnormality of internment. Throughout the book and even in *The Spanish Testament*, where Koestler faces death with many other ideologists, he never falters from the brute tension of reality. A quality which allows us to see Man suffering injustice, oppression, and death itself. Thus with such attitudes the writer could remark, 'The life we led was a proof of Man's capacity for adaptation. I think that even the condemned souls in purgatory after a time develop a sort of homely routine.'[13] The ironic humour is a testament to the human condition, and the writer's capacity for survival.

Brutus's strength in dealing with experience is uncertain. The most interesting contact of prison life is in homosexuality. By its very nature the sexual deviation illumines so much of what goes on underneath the façade of discipline. This the poet deals with tepidly and with veiled horror:

> Perhaps most terrible are those who beg for it,
> who beg for sexual assault.[14]

The strikingly prosaic arrangement, the allusion to 'it' and the repetition of 'who beg' shows a clear uncertainty, inability to face the point, in dealing with homosexuals. He is trying for emphasis, reassurance and self-conviction, but we feel this to be a result of the fear of becoming one of the perverted he describes. His reaction to 'Blue Champagne', the female homosexual (eighth letter) shows a distaste and horror, bordering on cruelty, which is almost final in its emphasis. According to the poet he is 'most perverse among the perverted' and therefore evil. Needless to say Brutus's 'fine' sense cannot come down to reality. It places him at a distance from the prisoners and their experiences.

We may well ask, what else can one expect in prison but such 'perversions'. The answer is given by a man, equally married to the concept of public opinion and life, and not very far from Brutus's own country and political climate. Of his general prison attitude, Kaunda could write, as **135** late as 1962, from his room in the Central Prison Salisbury, 'Prisons are dreadful places for anyone but they have their value for those of us who meddle in public affairs. There we see some of God's own children who need more care and attention than any others collected as often as courts of law sit. To me, these have a good case for demanding from us spiritual, moral and material care as much as a person struck down with acute pneumonia needs a physician . . . The prison is what we may describe as the headquarters of the underworld. It is a collection of people who themselves are one of the most challenging problems of mankind. This is true of prisoners all over the world I believe'.[15]

There is a totality of understanding here which is based on common sense and which is present in the prose, to which Brutus's poetry is rather a failing rival. With such intuition and with the stress on rising above the squalor imposed by the Salisbury racists and colonialists, it is no wonder that Kaunda felt and saw the interactions between Man and his prison environment far more clearly than Brutus can. 'When these poor boys come in for the first time (aged 15 to 20) they are so scared, they respond very quickly to anyone offering them protection and in many cases they will need it . . . If a boy tries to resist, his so-called protector arranges with others to thrash him so that by coming to the boy's protection at the right moment, he will submit to his unnatural desires. The organization of these incorrigibles is so effective, that warders will either explicitly or implicitly approve of the action. From this time, the boy is treated like a 'housewife'. Food as well as many other requirements in ordinary life which find their way into prison, in spite of the strict rules, the boy now receives.'[16]

Set next to the third letter to Martha, Kaunda's simple and very clear insight is far more credible than Brutus's explanation of violence and love in prison. In Kaunda's narrative just quoted we have a miniature of the whole prison system. The fear and insecurity of youth that leads to submission; the desire and lust of the older prisoners for protection and domination; the implicit concurrence of warders due to various 'needs'; the necessity for a 'housewife' in jail; the overall economic and social implications of the system. Hardly a glimpse of this extended world is to be got from Brutus's collection. His individual predicament and the fascist South African world both therefore merge to disappear into a distance, which makes the reader ask, 'Is poetry a suitable medium to convey the prison experience at all?' Through the effects of the overtones which Koestler and Kaunda achieve in their books, one feels that in jail men reason to retain their reason. Preoccupations with the self, therefore, though natural, are perforce kept at bay when prose is used to express thought and feeling. Brutus's continuous attempt to justify his own **136** rationale and the acutely prosaic arrangement of his verse betray the same kind of psychological process; only he has chosen a medium which inhibits him in a deadly way.

Granted that we may very well receive a more spontaneous outflow from verse than prose and that we should leave the poet to make us feel what *he* feels rather than impose our modes on him, yet do we find any quickness in Brutus's verse? Two significant attempts to respond to Nature in the last two letters to Martha indicate what I have in mind. The eighteenth letter seems to me quite contrived and in the main doubtful. There is an uneasy lack of seriousness which disturbs, which renders the confrontation between the prisoner and machine-gunning sentry melodramatic.:

> I scampered to the window
> and saw splashes of light
> where the stars flowered.[17]

Throughout the whole poem, the line that disturbs most is 'scampering to the window'. Can Nature be surveyed, responded to, and made the most of in such a hurry? In prison where time itself stands still? What does one glean from such an experience either about the poet or his environment? The sentry's barked warning to the prisoner when he plunged the cell into darkness to 'see' the stars, is as natural a reaction to such momentary foolhardiness, as our doubt of the poet's relationship to Nature. But it is really in the seventeenth letter that he betrays himself. The pathos of the poem verges on irritability, while a scientific description of the free flight of birds makes one question the very core of the poet's sensibility:

> the complex aeronautics
> and the birds
> and their exuberant acrobatics
> become matters for intrigued speculation
> and wonderment[18]

Where is the poetry here? The sense of distance which we need when thinking of the cloud or the bird are not present in the poem. In the lines above there is no feeling of the matchless freedom of flight and motion of birds, the appreciation of which would give the reader an awareness of the contrasting world of prison from where the poet writes. By comparison, Kaunda can give, albeit in an outdoor rather than an indoor prison, a description which carries the reader far more readily. The following passage is written at Camp Kabongo:

> Here I seemed to be nearer and nearer to understanding the language of Nature. I studied the various shapes of trees and this gave me great pleasure. As the quiet breeze blew from the River Kabongo the trees and **137**

the grass around seemed to dance to a strange tune which made me feel that I was in the midst of music which would never come the way of my ears. However, there I sat, while minutes ran into hours.[19]

The freshness of response is evident in the understanding that the largeness, the loneliness, and the non-humanness, of Nature around him is unique to the moment. Such an awareness from the writer necessarily makes the reader comprehend the larger background of words, ideas, speeches, agitation, and organization, in which Kaunda the politician lived; where Nature's untrammelled existence and soothing harmony would never be his. That is why it is a 'strange' tune. Yet for the moment it is eternally there for him and the reader, while time lapses into easily prolonged perspectives of 'minutes into hours'.

One of the functions of poetry is to ensure the survival of Art in man, to say the most probable things in the least number of words, and to make it as fresh in tone as the poet can. The repetitions in Brutus's verse, therefore, one must question. Everything that he says seems so strikingly familiar. Verse which contains no surprises indicates some essential flaw – either a language problem or an audience problem or just a blunted intuition. Here for instance:

> Cement – grey floors and walls
> cement – grey days
> cement – grey time
> and a grey sussuration[20]

The lack of compression is remarkable, the total effect prosaic, undermining the very mood it seeks to create. Even if Brutus was in solitary confinement, which as noted earlier is something we are not informed about, there must be more than just impression and visual effects that can be given the reader for his effort of reading. Almost the same feeling that Brutus seeks, is conveyed by Hammerskjöld in his own 'tower of confinement', through a combination that grows upon the reader like the feeling of darkness the poet wants to convey:

> Day slowly bleeds to death
> Through the wound made
> When the sharp horizon's edge
> Ripped through the sky.[21]

The sense of poured-out tension and emptiness (slow, wound, bleeding, death) is matched by the overwhelming violence of the last line, where we feel the darkness at one gulp swallowing the light and the writer. Compare also the mood of watchful suspense in the following image of Brutus:

> On Saturday afternoons we were embalmed
> in time like specimens of moths pressed under glass[22]

where the lifelessness of the chemically-treated moth automatically kills suspense, to Hammerskjöld's:

> Naked against the night
> The trees slept[23]

where the bareness of the atmosphere has a ready suspense, and the face of the writer is contained within the lines, looking at the chilly, frightful, landscape, inescapably drawing the reader along. Consider also the attempts to depict momentary finality by both poets. For Brutus, as visiting hour at the prison passes by, the feeling is:

> Until suddenly like a book snapped shut
> all possibilities vanished . . .[24]

and for Hammerskjöld:

> The cicadas shrieked
> As the glowing fire consumed
> Their last evening.[25]

Brutus's image is essentially archaic. The gesture of shutting the book does not close the mind from thought. But in Hammerskjöld the inverted order in nature (cicadas herald the evening) immediately suggests a momentary consummation, a feeling of natural light destroying insect life in one powerful sweep, with 'last' adding the final touch.

Finally, if it is thought that every writer's pen is bound to suffer in comparison with another's, let me point to the fact emerging out of his poetry that weakens the foundation of Brutus's verse. The poet's special designation 'coloured' has important implication in the South African situation. By such an intermediary arrangement, a man may belong in his own mind, to two races at once – 'black' and 'white', or to neither. But never to the third one, the 'human' race, that which is his own. In case this point is thought nebulous, the reader should refer to Ezekiel Mphahlele's story 'A Point of Identity'[26] where according to this recognized writer on the South African question, the life-springs of Karel Almeida, the hero of the story, go slack when he opts for 'coloured' instead of 'black' identity. The choice, partly enforced and partly self-orientated, takes him away from human brotherhood. We find Almeida sighing on his death-bed and communicating the following to the narrator, 'A black man like you T. can **139** go a long way. A black man has people around him to give him strength. I haven't.'[27]

Brutus, like Almeida, is not free from the cruel irony imposed by his racist government. He is unable to choose between the 'human' truths, of justice and freedom, and the 'racial' truths, which are continuous comparison and equivocation based on class and culture. There is besides a sense of underlying religiousness in his poetry which makes him suspect. Indeed the simplicity and earnestness of tone *is* religious. Whereas elsewhere this may be a positive or neutral quality, it is purely negative in South Africa – of the seventies. There is no greater deterrent to protest against outrageous tyranny than a religion of love.

Thus with reference to the colour question we find the following strange attraction by the poet, in the poem called 'The Mob', where a white crowd attacked the protesters against the Sabotage Bill:

> O my people
> O my people
> What have you done
> and where shall I find comforting
> to smooth awake your mask of fear
> restore your face, your faith, feeling, tears.[28]

It is legitimate to ask who are the poet's people and if they deserve his sympathy. The mob that attacked those who struggle for the minimal freedom in South Africa are literally faceless, faithless, and, as Dostoevsky said, without the gift of human tears. Yet the poet's refrain, 'O my people' gives his heart to them. Brutus even believes that when the white South Africans celebrate Blood River Day on 16 December:

> Their guilt
> is not so very different from ours.[29]

In three consecutive poems on pages 26, 27, and 28, he tries to deal with the day, which has special significance for the Boers. On this date, in the year 1838, they broke the Zulu military power of King Dingaan, Natal was secured, and Pietermaritzburg was established. Behind is the history of acute racial violence on black and white sides. Mistrust, broken contracts and what the Zulus thought was white man's witchcraft, are interwoven in the struggle for land and power. But according to Brutus the only difference between 'white South African guilt' and others, in the poem on page 26, is that the former is:

> On a social, massive organized scale
> which magnifies enormously.[30]

I find it difficult to accept this judgement based on size and numbers. His interpretation of guilt itself is questionable. Considering the attempted genocide on both sides in the 1830s, the history of such a situation is necessarily complex. Brutus's interpretation is not. He has chosen the 'safe' way of contrasting individual guilt complex based on misuse of personal power, greed, and instinctive temptation. But the history of the last two centuries of the West shows a gloomier picture. The massive drive for acquisition of wealth in African colonies, the acceptance and expansion of the slave system on a racial basis, the European's desire to flee from his own land and culture, of which the trekking, fighting, and settlement in South Africa was an organic part, all these show something very different from the guilt complex at work on a social scale, which the poet has in mind. History and poetry are gunpowder and light working together. In the limited space of short poems like Brutus's they have little room to be bed-fellows. But if they are forced into the situation, then the organizer of such a synthesis must somehow ensure a safe solution, which is what Brutus has done. In an epic on Blood River Day there could have been room for explosions and reflections.

This cleavage between right and wrong, which leads to the guilt complex, has a revealing interpretation in the hands of Norman Mailer, who went to prison for anti-Vietnam activity. It is the difference between 'religious' and 'artistic' guilt. For Mailer the friction engenders the will-power to go further than before, at all levels. In *Armies of the Night* he stated in the following form the interaction, in relation to sex and domestication, which he had temporarily to renounce to join the moral battle:

> For guilt was the existential edge of sex ... One advanced into sex against one's sense of guilt, and each time guilt was successfully defied, one had learned a little more about the contractual relation of one's existence to the unheard thunders of the deep – each time guilt herded one back with its authority, some primitive – hence some creative clue to the rages of the deep – was left to brood about ... which was a way of saying that nobody was born a man; you earned manhood provided you were good enough, bold enough.[31]

Thus in the hands of a man who has a professional understanding of life, the imposed conditions of growth and environment are an accepted front-line formation for the battle to develop a true individuality. It is the process of earning manhood, of self-discovery. The struggle, as can be seen from the style of the quoted passage, is genuinely complex, compulsory, and harsh. The acceptance gives Mailer the pre-eminence in American writing that he enjoys today.

It is not that Mailer is fighting in a free country. He also has two great enemies – the whole weight of American bureaucracy and the national **141** bourgeois conscience in which he too is enmeshed. Yet he triumphs in great discord rather than in an illusory peace. For Brutus on the other hand, when the nihilistic impulse, what Mailer calls 'the thunders of the deep', gets hold of him, he waters the fire at once, as seen in the eleventh letter:

'Voices shouting in the heart
"Destroy! Destroy!"
or
"Let them die in thousands!"
really it is impatience.'[32]

It is the prerogative of every free man, or one who is trying to be free, to indulge his ego to the maximum. The actual strength of the self is a test of prevailing social and cultural conditions. Thus it is that Mailer's work, because he believes in the self, in a free society, is so full of the outside world, while Brutus's is not. In an untitled poem, the latter comes so close to the doctrine of the other cheek that hardly anything positive may remain:

But it is best to shutter the mind and heart
eyes, mouth and spirit;
say nothing feel nothing and do not let them know
that they have cause for shame.[33]

'Them' and 'They' are relative here and it is uncertain in the whole poem what the pronouns refer to. Even the 'Old fighters' to which the pronouns seem to be connected, do not have any explicit sense. But the creed of submission and withdrawal that the poet expounds is very disturbing.

Temperamentally Brutus is unsuitable to take on the sophisticated might of the South African Government. This unsuitability leads to simplistic conclusions of hope without struggle. In two poems written on the day he left South Africa for the free world, there are revelations which show the poet pushing back the edge of experience for illusions. In 'To Canon Collins' he argues that Man's scientific prowess, his mastery over time and space, denotes a positive note, so that:

Pain shall be quiet, the prisoned free and
wisdom sculpt justice from the world's
jagged mass.[34]

In a sentimental farewell to South Africa he achieves a beatific vision for himself, on board the plane, with 'only the sky and air and light' around

him, which makes him feel:

Peace will come
we have the power
the hope
the resolution
Men will go home.[35]

But it is an ethereal vision, achieved only in a vacuum. The massive drive by Kaunda and Nyerere to try and persuade Heath to stop arming South Africa shows how difficult the struggle is at any one given point. But for me, the most damning lines in the whole collection are in the untitled poem where the poet discusses his role in the expulsion of South Africa from the Olympics:

Let me say it
for no one else may
or can
or will
or dare.[36]

Why should he feel so isolated? Why is it that 'no one' will recognize his role? Does it really need courage to say what he wants to say, so that he has to whip himself to such a tension before he can say it? The use of 'can', 'will', 'dare', in relation to 'no one' is mere rhetoric which does not befit the dedication of a fighter and is unworthy of the cause the poet is fighting for.

Yet in the end, despite the severe negligence of the publishers Dennis Brutus does express the cruel dilemma of a South African writer well. Those who can manage to, get out. But with family and relatives the persecuting authorities can take vengeance on them. This is difficult. Those who cannot get out may take their own lives or else sing for the government, or equivocate. Our mitigating impulse for such men is that those who have not tested the sweet fire of this free world of ours, can hardly do better. The poet and the publishers, their assumption of men and the reading public, will no doubt serve as an open warning to our understanding of South Africa for a while to come.

PUBLISHER'S NOTE   The collected verse of Dennis Brutus was published in 1973 after this article was written. It has the title *A Simple Lust* and together with new poems it includes *Letters to Martha*, *Sirens Knuckles Boots* and *Poems from Algiers* which have been previously published as individual editions. The sequence *Letters to Martha* has been rearranged by Dennis Brutus in chronological order.

NOTES

1. Nyerere, *Daily Nation*, 26 October 1970.
2. Brutus, *Letters to Martha* (Heinemann, London, 1968).
3. Brutus, *Sirens Knuckles Boots* (Mbari Publications, Ibadan, 1962).
4. Cope and Krige, *Penguin Book of South African Verse*, p. 17.
5. Brutus, *Letters*, p. 42.
6. Paul Theroux, *Introduction to African Literature*, ed. Ulli Beier (Longmans, London, 1967), p. 112.
7. Nkosi, *Home and Exile* (Longmans, London, 1965), p. 126.
8. Hammerskjöld, *Markings* (London, Faber and Faber), p. 175.
9. Brutus, *Letters*, p. 17.
10. Koestler, *Scum of the Earth* (Hutchinson, London, 1955), Front Jacket.
11. *Ibid.*, p. 113.
12. *Ibid.*, p. 154.
13. *Ibid.*, p. 126.
14. Brutus, *Letters*, p. 8.
15. Kaunda, *Zambia Shall Be Free* (Heinemann, London, 1962), pp. 131–2.
16. *Ibid.*, p. 133.
17. Brutus, *Letters*, p. 19.
18. *Ibid.*, p. 18.
19. Kaunda, *Zambia Shall Be Free*, p. 111.
20. Brutus, *Letters*, p. 38.
21. Hammerskjöld, *Markings*, p. 143.
22. Brutus, *Letters*, p. 39.
23. Hammerskjöld, *Markings*, p. 165.
24. Brutus, *Letters*, p. 39.
25. Hammerskjöld, *Markings*, p. 158.
26. Ezekiel Mphahlele, *In Corner B.* (East African Publishing House, Nairobi, 1967), p. 77.
27. *Ibid.*, p. 77.
28. Brutus, *Letters*, p. 36
29. *Ibid.*, p. 28.
30. *Ibid.*, p. 28.
31. Norman Mailer, *Armies of the Night* (Penguin Books, London, 1970), p. 35.
32. Brutus, *Letters*, p. 12.
33. *Ibid.*, p. 24.
34. *Ibid.*, p. 34.
35. *Ibid.*, p. 35
36. *Ibid.*, p. 50.

Naked Into Harvest-Tide: The Harvest Image in Soyinka's *Idanre*

Eldred D. Jones

The harvest image is the central one in 'Idanre'. It provides not only the overall framework but also much of the detailed machinery for the working out of the poem's themes. Apart from the word 'harvest' itself, which occurs frequently throughout the poem, images of growth, words like 'corn', 'melons', 'seed', 'ovary', 'cornucopia', 'palm fruit', 'kernel', 'oil', 'gourds', as well as images derived from the feasting which accompanies harvest, constantly echo the harvest image. Harvest is a culmination of the essential rhythm of life; the cyclical rhythm of the death of the seed, followed by growth, which in its turn leads inevitably to death even in the harvest. This particular aspect of harvest – its coincidence with death – appears elsewhere in Soyinka's work. 'Rust is ripeness', the paradoxical opening line of his poem 'Season' states it economically; while in the same poem the inevitable link between death and growth is equally briefly represented in:

> . . . Laden stalks
> Ride the germ's decay . . .

This link between harvest and death is more elaborately worked out in 'Idanre', another of Soyinka's global presentations of man the victim as much of his own nature as of his surrounding circumstances.

The poem is set in the context of harvest as it involves both men and the god Ogun, the god of harvest. Men prepare for the harvest, but so, unknown to the generality of men, does the god himself.

Men accept the harvest gratefully; theirs is an instinctive act of trust. They do not seek to pry into the secrets of the god; they merely bare themselves to receive his beneficence:

> And no one speaks of secrets in this land
> Only that the skin be bared to welcome rain
> And earth prepare, that seeds may swell

> And roots take flesh within her, and men
> Wake naked into harvest-tide. (p.62)

The human counterpart to the receptivity of the earth and its role in the harvest cycle is shown in the symbolic representation of the pilgrim's communion with Oya:

> And she swam an eel into the shadows, felt her limbs
> Grow live, the torrents ran within and flooded us
> A gourd rose and danced between – without
> The night awaited celebration of the crops –
> She took and held it to her womb. (p. 63)

The baring of 'skins' suggests a ritual act, but also more than hints at a certain superficiality in the act. The reluctance of the majority to pry or to look more deeply into things is even more explicitly expressed in a later section of the poem where men await the descent of the god 'sightless', 'incurious', and with eyes piously averted:

> Sightless eyes prayed haste upon
> His slow descent, incurious to behold
> The claws of day rip wide the weakened shutters
> Of a mind divine.
> . . .
> A child averts his eye from an elder's
> Nakedness . . . (p. 81)

Only the poet dares look on at the god's agony; only he sees the god achieve understanding, only he reaps the resulting harvest of understanding with the god. The poet's pilgrimage to see Ogun in his agony as he prepares to receive the sacrifice of harvest, provides the outer framework of 'Idanre'.

Ogun too has to seek his own absolution before he can preside over the harvest and give absolution to men; for he is the lord of the harvest:

> He comes, who scrapes no earthdung from his feet
> He comes again in Harvest, the first of reapers. (p. 62)

But before any glorious manifestation:

> . . . Ogun
> Sought the season's absolution. (p. 69)

It is into this private communion of a god, in the primaeval setting of Idanre that the poet, at some risk, intrudes:

> . . . I followed fearful, archives
> Of deities heaved from primal burdens. (p. 69)

Ogun's ritual and recurrent ('again') absolution is in atonement for his day of error when, blind with blood and wine, he had indiscriminately slaughtered his own people, the men of Ire who had invited him to be their king and fight on their behalf. This is the surface story, but the men of Ire also represent the human race whose fate it is to destroy themselves almost with the predicability of harvest. Indeed, the image of harvest is used most effectively in the depiction of Ogun's indiscriminate carnage. It is significant that the battle is obliquely introduced through an image of locusts destroying crops; a frustration of harvest. This image of devastation represents the waste of resources that is war; the very reversal of the associations of harvest:

> *Overtaking fugitives*
> *A rust-red swarm of locusts*
> *Dine off grains*
>
> *Quick proboscis*
> *Find the coolers*
> *Soon the wells are dry.* (p. 73)

This ushers in the more explicit devastation of men by Ogun. Ogun here represents the elemental force of creation as well as of destruction, a force which men release at their own peril. This they, the men of Ire, did when they invited the reclusive god to come down and fight for them. The resulting carnage is the pictorial centrepiece of the poem:

> His sword an outer crescent of the sun
> No eye can follow it, no breath draws
> In wake of burning vapour. Still they cry
>
> Your men Ogun! Your men!
>
> This blade he forged, its progress
> Never falters, rivulets on it so swift
> The blood forgets to clot. (p. 75)

In the middle of this gory, melodramatic, passage (the two sections quoted are only a small sample) is placed a passage which suddenly introduces an almost domestic poignancy, expressing as it does the human consequences of the vast destruction that is being depicted. For this passage Soyinka selects once again images of harvest, but of harvest gone wrong:

> There are falling ears of corn
> And ripe melons tumble from the heads
> Of noisy women, crying
>   Lust-blind god, gore-drunk Hunter
>   Monster deity, you destroy your men! (p. 75)

The harvest has been violated; the usual feasting, merriment, and worship, have been replaced by a scene of waste and confusion. The noisy women evoke a pathetic picture of hopeless, fruitless activity in the face of inevitable doom.

All this contrasts with the blend of order and thankful piety that the harvest ought to be, as other lines, placed after the bloody harvest, make clear:

> *The rams*
> *Are gathered to the stream*
> *For blessing*
>
> *Hour of prayer*
>
> *And curved horns curve*
> *Into hearts of the faithful*
> *The priest*
> *Cleansed his fingers*
> *In new springs*

This orderly harvest with the god in his heaven and the priest at his altar is the kind men hope for and pray for, but their own acts often deny them. The fault is not entirely their own, however. As in *The Swamp Dwellers* and *A Dance of the Forests* the gods are not blameless. Ogun had deserved the name 'cannibal', for he:

> . . . had dire reaped
> And in wrong season . . . (p. 84)

and consequently:

> . . . the children of Ogun
> Reaped red earth that harvest . . . (p. 71)

It is for this dire reaping that Ogun has to undergo his yearly penance.

Yet this is Ogun who, paradoxically, presides over the other kind of harvest; the fruitful, blessed harvest. It is he who causes the crops to grow. It was he who in the beginning had forged a path to earth to give the gods communion with men. Ogun's path is also the path of growth:

> Harvest night, and time to walk with fruit
> Between your lips, on psalming feet. We walked
> Silently across a haze of corn, and Ogun
> Teased his ears with tassels, his footprints
> Future furrows for the giant root. (p. 63)

This fusion of the essences of creation and destruction is part of Ogun's nature according to Yoruba mythology. He has come to symbolize in Soyinka's work the contradictions in man's nature. The poet's use of harvest as an image of destruction as well as an image of plenty and happiness in 'Idanre' is an apt artistic realization of this basic contradiction. This contradiction ushers into 'Idanre' a favourite theme of Soyinka's, namely the closeness of man in the exhilaration of speed in a motor car to the perpetual stillness of death, and the place of this sudden transformation in the inexorable cycle of growth/death/growth . . .

In the poet's walk to his communion with the god he passes a road with the usual reminders of car crashes. The wrecks having been stripped of spares are now playthings for children and (together with the remains of their human passengers) have become hot houses for new growth. The juxtaposition of death and life is pictured in a grimly witty passage:

> We walked through broken braids of steel
> And fallen acrobats. The endless safety nets
> Of forests prove a green deception
> Fated lives ride on wheels of death when,
> The road waits, famished
>
> Cave and castle, shrine and ghostly grottos
> Playthings now of children, shades
> For browsing goats. The wheels have fallen
> To looters and insurance men, litigant on
> Spare part sales and terms of premium
>
> The weeds grow sinuous through giant corrosions
> Skeletons of speed, earth mounds raised towards
> Their seeming exhaustion; growth is greener where
> Rich blood has spilt; brain and marrow make
> Fat manure with sheep's excrement (pp. 64–5)

Particularly in the last stanza quoted (the earlier stanzas depict harvests of their own) the image of growth has been pushed further, and now brings in a chilling constituent of the harvest – the cost of man's progress. Soyinka has now moved into a favourite theme, the harvest of the road. This is a harvest of man himself and his machine reaped by the 'famished' road, but a harvest which is the start of a further cycle, for the 'rich' blood fertilizes the growth of the weeds, and makes them healthier – 'greener'. There is also implicit in the stanza a levelling off of man by his portrayal as merely a part of the rhythmic natural cycle, his brain and marrow now fulfilling the same function as sheep's excrement, providing manure for the inexorable rhythmic cycle. This levelling off of man's body is somewhat compensated for later since the spirits of the dead, released in death, **149** join the ranks of the protective ancestors to preside over future harvests. The cycle is unending:

> ... They rose,
> The dead whom fruit and oil await
> On doorstep shrine and road, their lips
> Moist from the first flakes of harvest rain –
> Even gods remember dues.   (p. 65)

They are the guests who tomorrow will preside unseen, and 'To whom the rams will bow'.

Thus the cycle continues. Soyinka reinforces the harvest image with other images of continuity – Atunda's boulder, the wheel, the snake swallowing its own tail, rust producing growth, and (later) the 'Mobius strip':

> As the First Boulders, as the errant wheel
> Of the death chariot, as the creation snake
> Spawned tail in mouth, wind chisels and rain pastes
> Rust from steel and bones, wake dormant seeds
> And suspended lives.   (p. 65)

Plants, men, even gods, have their harvests. The absolution of Ogun is as rhythmic as the earthly harvest, and it is in this absolution of the god that the poet shares. The harvest he reaps is understanding, an understanding which is coincident with the god's own understanding:

> Light filled me then, intruder though
> I watched a god's excorsis; clearly
> The blasphemy of my humanity rose accusatory
> In my ears, and understanding came
> Of a fatal condemnation.
>
> And in that moment broke his crust of separation
> And the blood scales of his eyes.   (p. 79)

The vision which is the reward for the poet's daring to share in a god's 'pre-banquet' is unique. As is implicit in lines quoted earlier, most men do not seek to pry into the secrets of the gods; they accept the rhythms of life without questioning. Only the poet dares to pry into the essence of things. It is the lone artist – the man who dares to make the pilgrimage – it is he who hears 'the wisdom of the silence' which turns out to be (aptly) a celebration of the individual will. He learns, like the god, the lesson that in the manifestation of individuality is life, and in the gelling of all men into a shapeless homogeneity is death. Even Ogun has to learn this for he

150

had in his blindness lamented Atunda's act of splintering the original unified essence:

> Rather, may we celebrate the stray electron, defiant
> Of patterns, celebrate the splitting of the gods
> Canonization of the strong hand of a slave who set
> The rock in revolution – and the Boulder cannot
> Up the hill in time's unwind. (p. 82)

This knowledge which is the poet's harvest is not entirely a comforting one, for accompanying it is the waywardness of the human will, and the potential for destruction which activated the men of Ire. This is man's eternal risk. The boulder can never now be rolled back up the hill. Man lives in fear; lives in hope; the hope expressed in a vision of harvest – the kind for which he consciously prays and makes sacrifices; the kind which so often eludes him; the kind for which in his own country the poet still waits:

> The first fruits rose from the subterranean hoards
> First in our vision, corn sheaves rose over hill
> Long before the bearers, domes of eggs and flesh
> Of palm fruit, red, oil black, froth flew in sun bubbles
> Burst over throngs of golden gourds. (p. 85)

> And they moved towards resorption in His alloy essence
> Primed to a fusion, primed to the sun's dispersion
> Containment and communion, seed-time and harvest, palm
> And pylon, Ogun's road a 'Mobius' orbit, kernel
> And electrons, wine to alchemy. (p. 85)

COMMENTS

Ferdinand Oyono:
A Dissenting View

Mukotani Rugyendo

One is bound to have a lot of misgivings with regard to the interpretation that Jeannette Kamara (in *African Literature Today* No. 3) gives to Ferdinand Oyono's writing and particularly *The Old Man and the Medal*. While in a somewhat light manner she points out that *The Old Man and the Medal* has the rare quality 'of bringing together both the comic and the sad elements in the situation of pre-independence Africa', the points on which she lays her emphasis leave a lot to be desired and appreciated.

In her assessment of the 'chief value' of *The Old Man and the Medal*, Kamara asserts:

> Informative without being tedious, the novel is free of invective, polemic or whining self-pity. It contains all the elements so familiar to the African novel: the social gap between whites and blacks, colonizer and colonized, with the exploitation of the latter by the former, the African mistress carefully kept out of sight, and adequate criticism of a powerful and hypocritical church. But these are all etched in to provide sufficient background to a funny story.

And towards the end of her review, she concludes on the writer and his works:

> His chief aim has always been to entertain and, like *Houseboy*, this novel makes thoroughly enjoyable reading.

The main point here is for us to ask ourselves which of the two is the more **152** important in a work of art: the content or the form? I would rather think that it is the content. It is generally true that most writers have a philosophy of life or a message that they want to impart to their readers. No matter whether this philosophy is progressive or reactionary, Marxist or liberal, etc., it is still there. It is this which motivates a writer to say what he wants to say. Even those writers who cannot be said strictly to be having a particular philosophy of life still have something in their socio-economic set-up that prompts them to engage in diatribes, laugh sardonically, or whatever it is they might do. And any writer worth his salt selects his language, images, and general tone, according to how he thinks he will bring out what he wants to say most effectively. A responsible writer must certainly make his facts or philosophy readable – entertaining as such. He must lure the reader into reading his work, for literature in effect is a way of using man's capacity for enjoyment in order to educate him.

It is in this light that I look at Oyono as a writer. *The Old Man and the Medal* as Kamara rightly notes is about the colonial situation in pre-independence Africa but in an unspecified French colony – although one could be allowed to suggest that it is most likely Oyono's own Cameroon. The novel can in very many respects by likened to Chinua Achebe's *Things Fall Apart*. The social tragedy that has occurred in Doum, whereby the church has been used as a propaganda tool to enhance colonial administration, is very much like the overtly humiliating experience the people of Mbanta and later those of Umuofia in *Things Fall Apart* undergo.

The people of Doum are certainly aware of this tragedy. When in the first chapter Meka (the old man) stops at Mammy Titi's house on his way to the Commandant's residence the people he meets discuss it. Part of the conversation that specifically refers to Meka goes:

'. . . You're the one who gave your land to the Good Lord.'
'To the Catholic mission you mean,' someone corrected.
'What's the difference?'
'It comes to the same thing,' said Mammy Titi. (p. 7)*

And when Meka accepts that it was him, someone follows with, 'What a stupid sod.' Oyono goes on to comment on the awkward situation of Meka, the 'model Christian' in the Catholic mission at Doum through his sardonic humour and bitter irony. As a reward for giving away his land to the priests, Meka now lives in a small wretched hut 'at the foot of the Christian cemetery'. And given the chance to choose his place in the church he opts for bare cement covered with flies and reserved for beggars and kneels beside an aged leper. This is the real Oyono, the master of ironical twists of situation and language, a task in which he excels most other African writers.

* All page references to *The Old Man and the Medal*, translated by John Reed (African Writers Series, Heinemann 1969). **153**

He introduces this tragedy so early in the novel to show us his main pre-occupation – his chief aim as such.

The same tragedy bears an indelible mark in the words that the Commandant tells Meka a few hours later, as to why he is to receive a medal:

> 'You have done much to forward the work of France in this country. You have given your lands to the missionaries, you have given your two sons in the war when they found a glorious death.' (He wiped away an imaginary tear.) 'You are a friend.' (p. 19)

Jeannette Kamara emphasizes Kelara's initial joy and Meka's own happiness at the 'honour' more than the heaviness of this tragedy. We cannot do this unless we want to concern ourselves with their early deception in itself, which makes them fail to see the reality of things, rather than the ironical situation in which we see them as created for us by Oyono. We also have to note (as Jeannette Kamara points out in passing) the youth's comment as Meka waits for the 'honour' to be bestowed on him: '. . . To think he has lost his land and his sons just for that . . .' (p. 94), which immediately draws Kelara's realization to the essence of the situation and denies her peace ever after.

I am forced to differ from Kamara when she believes that it is the humour in *The Old Man and the Medal* which is of prime importance. For her, the joy of Meka and Kelara, which is but shortlived and ironical and which they experience before their eyes are opened, overshadows the social tragedy. It is strange to see Kamara highlight different bits of humour, as when Meka prays to God that he may be enabled to take off his painful shoes 'and have a piss . . .', and say that this is what there essentially is to the novel. I do not agree that the social tragedy is only meant to provide the story with sufficient background. Instead the reverse holds true. Oyono set out to comment bitterly on the tragedy and show how the people of Doum, and Meka in particular, eventually become better men who can see 'where the rain began to beat them' (to use Chinua Achebe's phrase). It is this new consciousness, this realization that they have all along been deceived by the church and the colonial administrators and their rejection of the professed brotherhood of whites, which epitomizes the importance of the novel. The humour is only thrown in by the writer to make the story readable and his statement on life realized.

As I note above, *The Old Man and the Medal* can in many respects be compared to Chinua Achebe's *Things Fall Apart* which deals with a more or less similar social tragedy – although the former is set at a point in the history of the society when colonialism is already a reality while the latter concerns itself with colonialism's advent to Africa. When Meka roars to his fellow men, 'You aren't men at all except that you've got a pair of balls! . . .' (p. 147), he is expressing his indignation at their emasculation by the colonial situation as Okonkwo expresses his own at the effeminate nature of the men of Mbanta and Umuofia in *Things Fall Apart*. The realization in *The Old Man and the Medal* that the whites had upset all the traditions of the land is like Obierika's view of the white man in *Things Fall Apart*: '. . . He has put a knife on the things that held us together and we have fallen apart.' It is interesting to note that Meka embodies the spirit of the entire Doum society just as Okonkwo is the embodiment of the same in Umuofia. The people agree that what has happened to Meka (being imprisoned and humiliated by the whites he formerly thought were brothers) has happened to all of them through him.

Jeannette Kamara's view on the 'sociological' aspect of the novel also needs clarification. It is true that in the course of the change between the traditional African values and the new French standards, the emphasis on the position and values of the 'real' man has shifted. This can be even easily explained on the light family level. If a man imposes himself on the family of another man and dominates him, then the dominated man can no longer be called a 'real' man. In fact in many traditional African societies he is referred to as a woman. So much, therefore, for the shift in meaning under colonialism – and it is a real shift. It is also true that notions of 'negritude' and 'African identity' develop as the eyes of the dominated African are opened and he seeks to throw out the enslaver. And since in imposing himself the colonialist has developed myths about the African and his culture to demoralize him, then the African hits back with a similar force drawing on his rich cultural heritage, exposing the lies of the colonizer and creating a base from which to fight. One cannot fight without the right morale. Jeannette Kamara and the 'unsympathetic critic' she quotes need to know that 'negritude' does not mean 'the uglier, the better'. This is a distortion that has developed as all sorts of hypocritical and even irrational exponents of the philosophy have come on the scene. True 'negritude' simply means the attempt on the part of the colonized black man to rehabilitate his civilization and gain the necessary equilibrium so that he can assert himself effectively. And in this regard the kind of 'manhood' and 'real' man assertions found in a lot of novels by African writers are in their own way negritudist. *The Old Man and the Medal* ranks very high among these.

True artists always have a philosophy of life that seeks to put things the right way up in the socio-economic and socio-political structure. And here, Ferdinand Oyono feels very bitter about French colonialism in Africa, exposes the hypocrisy behind the professed brotherhood of the whites and particularly the cassock-attired Catholic Fathers and shows the African emerging out of this mysticism and deception as a better man, who **155** certainly can never be hoodwinked again. Oyono only introduces the humour, a lot of which is sardonic, to execute his task more effectively and give an entertaining story. To think and assert that Oyono's statement on life is less important than the fun and humour is to trivialize the whole thing, and to miss the main point for which Oyono should be given high credit. His chief aim has always been to expose the evils of the colonial situation.

Answer to Rugyendo's article

Jeannette Kamara

Mr Mukotani Rugyendo's review of my review of *The Old Man and the Medal* by Ferdinand Oyono is interesting enough in its way, and even useful to those who persist in reading Black African Literature from a purely socio-political angle.

It is true that many of our black writers are primarily concerned with form rather than with content, assuming, as Mr Rugyendo does, that the two elements can be separated and treated in isolation. Yet the fact remains that the manifesto is properly the medium for the socio-political testimony. And Oyono's merit as a writer is that he is in control of his art, of his subject, and of his emotions where the black man's tragic colonial predicament is concerned. He sees, and rightly, that if he is to write a story he has to make his ideas develop out of the characters and situations he creates.

True, he is concerned with the burning humiliation, the emasculation of the black man's manhood by the white colonial master – but at the same time he can watch a cockroach wander around on Meka's precious helmet. He can show Meka, a figure of ridicule in his bizarre western-type clothes, dying to have a piss. All this because Oyono's depiction and denunciation of white colonialism in Africa is subtle and implicit rather than flat and explicit. And most important, Oyono has not lost his sense of humour. He has, like Mongo Beti, the rare quality of being an African who can laugh at himself. He can stand at a remove from his condition and see the humorous side of the whole business. That is assuming that Oyono, the writer, makes a personal identification with Meka or that there is a biographical element in the story, and we have no evidence of this.

Oyono seems to emphasize the tragedy of individuals such as Meka and Toundi (in *Houseboy*) by using comic understatement. He plays down the tragic elements of the situation and presents them in a humourous light. But while we, as readers, are smiling over the incongruity of the various situations, the sensitive among us will understand and appreciate the literary skill and maturity of Oyono in this different presentation of old and well-worn themes.

Oyono has written a story to entertain as well as instruct the reader, and if the story is not entertaining will the reader read long enough, or closely enough, to be instructed? To look at *The Old Man and the Medal* principally as a social document would be to diminish Oyono's reputation as a storyteller in the tradition of a Daudet or a Somerset Maugham. For to what extent can we separate the story from the medium of its presentation?

The critic who attempts to separate the idea from the language runs the risk of never grasping the work as a rounded whole. Oyono did write about a tragic situation but he did present this in its humourous element. Who are we to dismiss such a functional aspect of his work? And further, who are we to put to rights in our criticism what we feel Mr Oyono wrongly to have underplayed?

REVIEWS
Jared Angira

Bahadur Tejani

Jared Angira, *Juices*: Poems, East African Publishing House, Nairobi, 1970

Juices is an uneven exciting collection. On the jacket we are informed that Mr Angira is a B.Com. from Nairobi. I mention this because for a poet so young, he speaks with a strikingly old voice.

Hence the unevenness. The collection includes verse with traditional themes, situations and character; straightforward narratives or descriptions which are poetically uncomplex, unsensuous or thought-provoking, though with a pastoral nostalgia interwoven successfully. 'Peninah Aloo' woman in rural setting by the lake, 'Dusk on My Village' an aware but unpolished sketch, 'On market Day At Ugunja', 'Last Words of a Father', and 'Kisumu' fall into such a group. Here the titles make the themes and situation apparent and comment is unnecessary.

On the margin of this tradition-consciousness and rural background, the poet flirts with cultural problems. 'The Undressing', 'Your Homecoming' and 'A Child of No World' portray men and women dislocated from bonds of older relationships. The men because of new ideas and books, the women a victim of forces of westernization by way of dress and fashion. In 'Soliloquy' Angira reshapes the concept of negritude. 'Black' for the poet is the scent of flowers, the shimmer of the sea, the fire of the artist and the moodiness of the dusk. This naturalization and psychologizing is a new and welcome approach, though diffused. 'Black' is also a long flight of imaginative challenge:

> Who goes with my shivering hands
> and hopeful heart
> beyond the unshapen clouds?

This sentiment is echoed in the opening poems where the flush of creativity confronts the idea of discipline. There is undaunted adolescence and innocence in the assertion;

> I own a superb choir
> made up of birds
> my house is lit by planets and not
> the unsettled fireflies.

158 The challenging tone also leads him to question the concept of justice in

'The Final Judgement' and time in 'Cavalcade'.

It is where the poet has actually committed himself to value judgements that he is most successful. 'Dry Tears', 'Masked', 'The Years Go by', 'An Evening Show', and 'Rape I' have strong political resolutions. Dealing with the nature of freedom and progress he questions and revalues by establishing a view-point and by satire. Of the loud-mouthed politicians Angira writes:

> Everyday they have acted
> and left the stage
> but only parrots
> have learnt their morals.

Social irony plays a part in 'Mtwappa Ferry' and 'The Palmwine Tapper' where an experiment with Marxian economics is conducted to present the poet's view of exploitation – especially in 'Fort Jesus' where a reinterpretation of history is achieved. Concern for social ills is felt in the 'Prostitute', 'a nestless bird that enters any nest' and in 'The Model', though the latter is rather sentimental.

Right at the end, the eager boisterous voice of youth breaks through in two of the loveliest poems of this side of Africa, 'Grandmother' and 'Rescue', which I am sure will be schoolboy's favourites overnight. It shows how full a poet Mr Angira can be when his idiom and theme come together. There is a delicacy of language and organization, and poetic pride that is matchless. Angira's description of the rural women carries positive echoes which are unique in East Africa:

> She
> Whose eyes twinkle like blue water
> gently cascading among tall reeds
> by a gentle fall
> on some smooth grey rocks
> she whose teeth are as white as cattle egrets
> as white as Kilimanjaro's crown
> whose tender skin
> is as smooth as a long-used milk gourd
> whose tapering legs
> downwards dove tail
> like the 'yago' fruit . . .

Depending on individual taste, the poems will yield very different results. Their range is wide. The poet's own obvious concern invites the reader to a similar involvement with issues. But the cleavage between the old and new must be solved before his idiom is refined to a sharpness which can adequately deal with his credo. 'Yet the shadow of Karl Marx seems to give my trembling self some consolation' as he says in the introduction. Marx and verse are a difficult combination. **159**

Okot p'Bitek

Bahadur Tejani

Okot p'Bitek, *Two Songs*: 'Song of Prisoner' and 'Song of Malaya', East African Publishing House, Nairobi, 1971.

Produced in a lovely white and red jacket, with the two faces of the prostitute and the prisoner evoking a harrowing harmony, Okot's latest compositions are a demonstration of the amount of matter a truly creative hand can pack into a very brief space. The publishers have altered their style of publicity as well, to suit the poet's originality. Instead of the usual prosaic piece at the back, there is an evaluating comment with the emphasis on connotative use of language. Eleven enticing illustrations by Trixi Lerbs, in the right places, make this volume compulsory possession. The only major complaint from the reader's point is the price. Who is going to buy Okot's work? One thought he was famous enough now for the publishers to take a risk and produce ten to fifteen thousand copies for the first edition to bring the price down.

Okot's prisoner is a vagrant in the city, and his first question as he lies beaten and torn behind bars is:

> Brother,
> How could I . . .
> A young tree
> Burnt out
> By the fierce wild fire
> Of Uhuru . . .
> Inspire you
> To such heights
> Of Brutality.

In section after section, the irresistible, plaintive, rich, hungry voice of mad ecstasy draws us on, pleading for justice. It is the 'cry of his children' with bellies 'drumming the sleep off their eyes'; the 'fiery lips of his sister's song'; the 'helpless ululation of his mother'; the cold body of his wife rocking 'with grief and regrets'; it is the voice of a clan surrounded by 'steel rhinoceroses and roaring kites sneezing molten lead and splitting the skies' with bombardment. It is the call of the common man for justice and for revenge, a defiance of the power-laden bellow of the chief's dog growing fat on people's labour:

> Listen to the Chief's dog
> Barking like a volcano,
> Listen to the echoes
> Playing on the hillsides!
> How many pounds
> Of meat
> Does this dog eat
> In a day?
> How much milk . . .?

The dog is the perfect symbol to expose the Chief's alienation from society, for only when man wants to barricade himself from his own kind, does he use this savage species as a means of protection. Later in one of the loveliest passages he has composed so far, the poet evokes the image of the Big Chief himself, breaking into the prisoner's home, riding his wife. Our sight, smell, sound and sense of movement combine to form this memorable picture created by a mind always exploring the language for fresh meaning.

> A black Benz
> Slithers smoothly
> Through the black night
> Like the water snake
> Into the Nile,
> Listen to it purring
> Like a hopeful leopard,
> Listen to its
> Love song,
> The soft poem
> That embraces the valleys
> And caresses the hills . . .
>
> The grasses on
> The pathway
> Hiss in protest
> The shrubs scratch
> Its ribs
> With their nails,
> Foxes hit the windscreens
> With their laughter,
> Dogs whine

And sharpen their teeth,
The gods riddle the car
With yellow arrows
Of starlight. . . .

The combined efforts of natural, animal, and spiritual life are powerless
in preventing the soft caress of the Wabenzi from spreading itself. This
theme is not new to East Africa. But the poet's style and rich imagery
expresses the contrast between the haves and have-nots in an entirely new
manner. Implicit in the lines is the ruthless mercenary power of the politician, his quiet hunting style, his capacity for sacrilege. As the exploiter's
fingers reach the very centre of his life, the prisoner demands revenge in
words that have the terror of the French guillotine in them.

I want to drink
Human blood
To cool my heart,
I want to eat
Human liver
To quench my boiling thirst,
I want to smear
Human fat on my belly
And on my forehead.

Here Okot speaks for all the wretched of the earth. Indeed in his
dream, the prisoner actually imagines himself shooting and destroying
'The sharks of Uhuru that devour their own children'. But in section nine
the poet's humanity, while justifying the action of the prisoner, consoles
the widow of the Big Chief.

In the last five sections of the poem, Okot tries a complex experiment,
of contrasting the inner life of a 'Minister' with that of the prisoner. Somehow this doesn't quite come off, simply because it's difficult to judge who is
who. One also feels the Minister's portrait to be a stereotype, though once
again, in the description of the prisoner's clan-life, proud and dignified like
the 'colourful cattle egret', there is excellence.

In the last two sections, the poem takes another turn. The dream is over.
The futility of protest, a voice shouting in the wilderness for justice and
revenge, is understood, accepted. The poet's plea seems to suggest that at
least if we can't have social and political justice, let's have the freedom of
spirit to sing and dance. This is what is claimed in the synthesis, which
follows Okot's usual anthropological bent, of combining various cultures:

I want to dance the dances
Of our friends and
The dances of our enemies,

I want to lift their daughters
To my shoulder
And elope with them . . .
. . . Let me dance and forget
For a small while
That I am a wretch,
The reject of my Country,
A broken branch of a Tree
Torn down by the whirlwind
Of Uhuru.

Yet if Okot's verse is to sell here and not in U.K., or U.S.A., if it's African ears who are to feel the twang of the social and political injustice, and not foreign mouths which are to savour the fantasies of his rich imagery, if the poet is to belong to us and not to them, E.A.P.H. had better look into their accounts again. Give us more Okot and give it to all of us, not the big chiefs only.

There is no discipline better suited than anthropology when you want to destroy the reading public's concept of morality.

Okot has given his historical and cultural sense full play in the malaya's song, which explodes all our sacred notions of good and bad.

The composition is one of the most daring challenges to society from the malaya's own mouth, to see if we can stand up to her rigorous scrutiny of ourselves.

The prudes, the puritans, and the respectable, have always frowned upon the street-walker, the adulteress, the courtesan, the malaya. But the history of sexual deviation, of perversion, seduction, and temptation, it is as old as man himself, embracing, according to the poet, the great names in world history.

The sly glance and the sensuous laugh is in the shanty of the slum, the royal bed, the appetite of Eve, and in the action of the acolyte near the saint, so claims the malaya:

Listen, Sister Prostitutes
In the Hilton suites.
Fill your glasses
With champagne . . .
And you in the slums
Distilling illegal gin . . .
Here's to Eve
With her golden apples.
And to the Egyptian girl
Who stole Abraham from Sarah's bed . . .
We'll drink to the daughter of Sodom
And to the daughter of Gomorrah

163

Who set the towns ablaze
With their flaming kisses . . .
Let's drink to Rahab
With her two spy boy friends,
To Esther the daughter of Abigail,
To Delilah and her bushy-headed
Jaw bone gangster,
To Magdalena who anointed
The feet of Jesus!
We will remember Theodora
The Queen of Whores . . .
And the unknown prostitute sister
Who fired Saint Augustine
To the clouds.

In the malaya's philosophy, Christianity, that supporter of the sexless,
is given special treatment. The poet creates a warm human picture of
mother-malaya waiting for the return of her school child. Upon the
discovery that the lad has been dubbed a bastard, her wisdom lets itself
loose upon our fundamentals.

Now, tell me
Who was the greatest man
That ever lived?
The saviour
Redeemer
The light . . .
King of Kings
The Prince of peace . . .
What was His Father's name?
Was the Carpenter
Really His Father?

And a pertinent question is put to the teacher:

How many teenagers
Have you clubbed
With your large-headed hammer.
Sowing death in their
Innocent fields?

The malaya's song is for everyone. The sailor coming ashore with 'a
time bomb pulsating' in his loin, the released detainee with 'granaries full
to overflow', the debauching Sikhs at the nightclubs with heads broken
open, and the vegetarian Indian 'breeding like a rat'.

The schoolboy lover is given a concession for the 'shy smile on his face'
so long as he does not swap tales with the teacher who was there last night!

The bush-teacher, chief, business executive, factory workers and shop assistants, party whips and demagogues, will all line up at her door to quench their thirst.

Okot's merciless satire takes toll of a whole humanity and the political mercenary collects the largest part of the whiplash on his groin.

> Oh-ha-ya-ya!
> But you were drunk,
> You could not finish . . .
> You feigned sleep.
> Snoring like a pregnant hippo . . .
> Your silly baby tortoise
> Withdraw its shrunken skinny neck . . .
> Leaving me on fire
> The whole night long. . .!

The big chief's impotency is matched only by the dark frustration of the family man. In one of the illustrations we see his pumpkin-bosomed wife, with a waistline like a barn door, ranting while a bunch of skinny children shiver at the hut's entrance.

No wonder the mini-skirted malaya, with breasts arched like the under-belly of the Concorde, is a relief for his soul. Automatically with such pleasure and brightness goes the poet's question: 'How dare you blame the gay-time girl?'

The malaya because of her intricate and wide experience of men, can teach the house-wife a thing or two.

> Come on Sister.
> Do you think
> Your wild screams
> And childish sobs
> Are sweet music
> In the ears of
> Our man?

The irony of the last line, of course, works both ways, for the malaya as well as the well-wedded wife.

The total effect of this intimate, seductive voice of the malaya is as illuminating as a thunder-flash in the silent night. Her rancour, her claims, her knowledge of men's ways and movements are unsurpassable. Through her, Okot explores the essence of guilt and shame that we harbour in ourselves.

The malaya is sharp enough to have facts and situations at her finger-tips she knows how to silence her brother's sham morality by pointing out who it was that shared a bed with her friend next door two nights ago. **165**

The sergeant who calls her a vagrant carries the 'battleaxe' with which he wounded her last night. For her and her kind, the cycle of the geisha is as natural as the rise of the morning sun and its dip in the west at dusk.

The bouncing vigorous voice of the malaya has enough intelligence and humour for her song to get the listener at one go.

> Black students
> Arriving in Rome,
> In London, in New York
> Arrows ready, bows drawn
> For the first white kid

The imagery is superbly hilarious, as when

> The wife
> In house
> Eats lizard eggs
> To prevent pregnancy!

Or when disease has made some inexperienced fool run mad, the courtesan adjusts her focus kindly for him

> Let the disappointed
> Shout abuses at us.
> Let them groan, sleep
> Their spears vomiting butter,
> Their buttocks swollen
> After the doctor's caning

Poets from Ghana

D. S. Izevbaye

Albert W. Kayper-Mensah, *The Dark Wanderer: poems*, Horst
Erdmann Verlag, Tübingen, Federal Republic of Germany, 1970.
Messages: Poems from Ghana, edited by Kofi Awoonor and
G. Adali-Mortty, Heinemann, African Writers Series, London,
1970.

Apart from being by Ghanaians, the poems in both these volumes are
similar in the way the presentation takes advantage of the varied African
and European influences. In the first volume Kayper-Mensah, the
Ghanaian poet-diplomat in Bonn, gives pride of place to Germany. The
tributes in the first section go to:

> The people of Beethoven and of Bach,
> The two who speak most clearly
> The language of the soul surprised
> By joy.

The verse has the competence and easy flow to be expected of a practised
writer, but its main strength is its concreteness. A moral or an aesthetic
experience is given concrete interpretation: Bach's music is a fertile field
crowded with tall plants weighed down by fruit; despair is the experience
of the:

> Emotional invalid, alone,
> Seeing life as a slipping
> Into defeat through the films of tears . . .

The verse is frequently imagistic, as in this picture of the Black Forest:

> Pine leaves in the dusk
> Are frozen splashes of black
> Ink, hanging, unmoving,
> On stiff straight branches.

167

The landscape often has a symbolic value, perhaps because of a certain ethical obsession. One poem has 'energies of spring' and 'winter of destruction'. The occasional ordinariness of sentiment is compensated for by the rhythmic brilliance of lines like these ones from 'Bad Aibling in Late Autumn':

> Your leafing love is over.
> Your autumn beauty, but a dying swan;
> Yellowing leaves browning into death.

The first section of the volume is made slightly monotonous by its tributes, and by the tendency to smuggle in a moral point whenever the poet gets a chance. 'At Todtmoos' tends towards a keep-our-city-clean campaign by its enthusiasm for a model Black Forest village, and the brave flicker of a line like 'a dying boy fading from his mother' is nearly smothered by a moralizing which belongs more properly to the two sections on 'Reflections'.

The poems about Africa are linked to those in 'Germany' and 'Reflections' by the frequency of the gnomic form and the witty opening in which an abstract quality is defined in concrete terms: 'Death is a strong broom / Made by God himself / And it will sweep us yet away'. The descriptive skill which marks the Germany group is brought into effective use in 'African Masks' where the language is as restricted as the wood which controls a sculptor's style:

> Pillars pop as eyes
> Fall as nose. . . .
>
> Cheeks pull out and up
> Upper lips stiffen
> Into joy smiling
> And what they say
> Is black or white
> But never grey.

The fondness for short lines in *The Dark Wanderer* sometimes betrays the poet into a jingle. Although the poet's nationalism is pressed too far in the use of untranslated vernacular lines, it is in the 'Africa' poems more than in the others that one expects new lines of development in his verse.

The vernacular tradition is by no means the only opening for a poet. The important thing is the range of expression which he can get out of a well-worn theme. This is well shown in *Messages*, the first of several regional collections of poems being published by Heinemann Educational Books. Many of the poems in this volume are variations on familiar themes
168 – childhood, nationalism, racial injustice, and the devaluation of Europe.

Many of the themes receive new handling, however. Duodu's 'Return to Eden' does not deal directly with the biblical garden or with a political utopia; it recalls the process of growing up and the consequent loss of innocence, in an attempted satire on the adult world.

The keynote for most of the poems is struck in the notes provided by Joe de Graft and Kofi Awoonor who, in their different ways, refuse to be pigeon-holed. The value of exercising this traditional poetic freedom is apparent in the method of the poems. It results in a successful fusion of ideas from Jung, the Bible, and modern technology, in an image like 'old psalms recorded on sound tracks through Adam's mind'. Or a poet might prefer a purely scientific utterance, as when de Graft describes contemporary violence as a genetic disease acquired by Time in an infectious contact with Science.

The poets in this volume have thus set themselves different conditions for practising the poet's art. Their literary conventions come from Europe or from Africa. As a symbol of mourning Sey uses a cypress and Awoonor a capsized canoe. The practice is, however, vulnerable in the first case because it implies a reliance on a mainly literary experience. One finds more meaning in Parkes's biblical verse in spite of its straining for effect, than in a poem like 'The Vampire' which seeks to make kinky black hair stand on end with the bogey of Dracula. A biblical foundation at least provides the type of meaningfulness to be found in 'Apocalypse' where the images of the roaring hare and the ape in a palanquin would be absurd if taken literally.

Language is more than a mere literary skill, it is a way of life. Adali-Mortty's 'Belonging' defines the problem of language with reference to social experience:

> You may excel
> in knowledge of their tongue,
> and universal ties may bind you close to them;
> but what they say, and how they feel –
> the subtler details of their meaning,
> these are closed to you and me forever.

It may not be easy to verify this claim, but this is surely the most telling message in the collection. Poetry as eloquent speech which touches the soul of a people should touch their lives as lived. In 'Nation Feeling' Kayper-Mensah argues for a sense of belonging:

> as Ghanaians
> Nourished by the sounds, sights, tastes
> Stimulations of home
> Rooted in a home manure.

169

More than anything else this is what lends vitality to the verse of Awoonor whose experiments with the traditional dirge are well known. The form is used effectively in 'Purification', a lament for a 'fish' who drowns. Significance is given to everyday statements through ironic emphasis:

> They didn't forget to place the sacrificial cow
> On the bow of the storm-experienced canoe
> Anipaye the fish, I shall stay at the net's end
> While you go down.
> While you go down.

The new phase of his poetry retains the communal concerns of his earlier work and the same tone of distress. But there is a new compression in 'Messages' where the images are absorbed into the verbs.

Pathos, humour, satire, rage, and even protest, are all present in *Messages*. It is altogether a balanced picture of what has been done and what is being done, with glimpsed promises of what is to come, although it is possible that the reader will notice the silence of new writers like Aidoo, Apronti, and Okai, whose voices he has heard elsewhere.

South African Poets   *Clive Wake*

Seven South African Poets, Selected by Cosmo Pieterse, Heinemann, African Writers Series, London, 1971.
Mazisi Kunene, *Zulu Poems*, André Deutsch, and Africana Publishing Corporation, New York, 1971.

The seven poets represented in Cosmo Pieterse's volume are all exiles from South Africa, driven out by the single-minded inhumanity of apartheid. It is the sort of experience that is bound to produce protest, and for these poets, protest came before exile and resulted in exile. Cosmo Pieterse wonders whether South African poetry is not therefore likely to become 'shrill, hysterical, thinly disguised political propaganda'. Certainly as regards the seven poets whose work he has offered to us, this is far from being the case. The one thing that strikes one very forcibly about these

poets is the complete absence of hysteria, the great reserve and the withholding of passionate outburst, which give the poems their power and convince the reader, very deeply, of the reality of the suffering they tell of – the suffering of imprisonment in South Africa, and all the other forms of deprivation apartheid brings with it; the suffering, particularly, of exile, which is in some ways perhaps the most difficult to bear. There is a noticeable lack of rhetoric in these poems, because they are written from actual experience. They are far from the rhetorical polemic, however masterly and impressive it is, of a David Diop, far from the intellectual meditations on heroism, leadership and culture – since there is time and space for them – of a Senghor.

In the poems of Dennis Brutus, for example, the effect is achieved by the simple descriptive account of an event, without intellectual elaboration or emotional embroidery, as in the poem 'En Route', which describes a truckload of men being carried off to prison, or in the next poem, 'They Backed the Truck', describing the arrival at the prison. In the first of these poems, Brutus gives the incident its universal dimension in the last line with an image which turns a simple fa;t into an idea:

> while from the dusk flowered the friendly faces.

In the second of these poems, the same effect is achieved by an unemphatic, but deeply evocative calling to mind of the whole history of South Africa:

> The old building
> with the mannerism of a bygone air
> exuded age, reeked history
> And we too were history.

This descriptive approach is found in other poets of this collection, as for example Dollar Brand's evocation of the misery of Cape Town's District Six, the ghetto of the Coloured community, or in this same poet's almost surrealistic, yet strongly realistic, piece, 'The Harmonica'. Or there is the visual irony of I. Choonara's two-line poem, which sums up so much of the South African situation:

> Oh, to be free, white, and twenty-one;
> Now that the jacarandas are in bloom.

Exile does, of course, have its own peculiar effect on the poetry these poets write. The evocation of incidents and scenes set in South Africa, however cruel and sad, the recollection of places, things, activities, and people, that have been left behind, inevitably have their dimension of nostalgia. It works the opposite way, too; the peace and beauty, the freedom, of the English countryside intensifies Dennis Brutus's feeling for **171** those who are still in South African prisons. Exile also frees the mind from its constricting obsession with the South African situation when one lives it from the inside; poets in exile are able to relate their South African experience to the tragic situations in which others find themselves, in Vietnam (I. Choonara, 'Letter to Mamma') or in Hiroshima at the time of the atom bomb (Arthur Nortje, 'Hiroshima 21 and the Lucky Dragon'), and to recognize that others suffer as well, that evil has universal dimensions. While C. J. Driver points to the complexity and the agony of choices the man of conscience has to face in South Africa, in his poem 'To the Dark, Singing', 'in memory of John Harris':

> The flame burns white in his skull
> And no one death repeats another.

There is, in fact, a variety of themes and styles in this slim volume. Keorapetse Kgositsile writes the most obviously political poems, but also some fine love poems; C. J. Driver reflects on politics, the effect of the South African situation on his white university contemporaries, and on death; Timothy Holmes has a fascinating obsession with birds and animals. The poems are serious, ironic, humorous. There is a variety of free verse, and some blank verse, and a command of both (I. Choonara is particularly impressive). The language has, for the most part, a directness which is highlighted by contrast with the somewhat over-elaborate quality of Arthur Nortje's style.

Mazisi Kunene's *Zulu Poems* are very different. Originally written in Zulu, they come over remarkably well, for the most part, as English poems. In his introduction, the poet explains their place in the Zulu oral poetic tradition, of which he sees them thematically and stylistically very much a part and a continuation. To appreciate them fully, he tells us, the English reader must approach them from the point of view of the Zulu world-picture. As far as the theory, at least, is concerned, his views are very reminiscent of Senghor, and so too is much of his imagery:

> Years come carrying firewood on their heads.

But writing as he does in Zulu, in so far as the language of the people is deeply rooted in its past as well as its present in a way Senghor's French is not, Kunene conveys a strong impression of the realness of this world-picture, even though from the outside and via an English translation, one may have a stronger feeling of a certain anachronistic quality, of its growing irrelevance in the hard modern westernized world. For this reason, poems

172 that are clearly very traditional, such as 'Conquest at Dawn', make little impression on the non-Zulu reader. On the other hand, many of the poems rise above the accidents of regional tradition, and through the local imagery proclaim a universal message. There is a great deal of the serenity of traditional African wisdom in many of these poems. There is also an awareness of human weakness, of man's inhumanity to man, of the inevitability of death. Such for example is the piece entitled simply 'A Poem':

> May I when I awake
> Take from all men
> The yearnings of their souls
> And turn them into the fountain of Mpindelela
> Which will explode into oceans;
> Not those of the south that are full of bitterness
> But those that are sweet to taste.

The African languages reflect a culture which has, at least until recently, been much aware of the reality of the natural world, so that nature in these poems is not used to create mood, as in much European poetry, but is a direct reflection of the realities of life. Much like the poets of the modern French surrealist tradition, the African poet sees nature as a reality, not as metaphor, as a series of correspondences, not as simile. In this respect, Kunene's imagery is very reminiscent of that of his *confrère*, Jean-Joseph Rabéarivelo, who lived and wrote and was inspired by the countryside of his island of Madagascar, a neighbour of Zululand:

> And the suns are torn from the cord of the skies
> And fall to the ground humiliated by the cluster of leaves.
> The eternal feet travel on on their journey.
> The bars of iron pierce through, feeding on their blood.
> The wedding party walks proudly
> And catches a glimpse of the moon disintegrating.
> . . .
> Knowing how because of us,
> We who are the locusts with broken wings,
> Our shadows shelter the earth from the sun.

Kunene joins up with the poets of the Pieterse volume in a number of poems attacking the South African system, with the same restraint, the same preference for understatement, the same overriding awareness of humanity. There is, indeed, in the humanism of the poets of both these volumes, in their dignity and, one might almost say, in their serenity, a core of hope and reality which holds out some promise for the inhuman, somehow unreal, horror of the South African situation.

Wole Soyinka
Eldred Durosimi Jones

Wole Soyinka, *A Shuttle in the Crypt*, Rex Collings/Eyre/Methuen, London, 1972.

Soyinka's great quality as a poet is his ability to distance an immediate experience through the selection and deployment of expressive images. This quality was amply demonstrated in his earlier volume, *Idanre and Other Poems*. The more harrowing the experience, the more valuable this ability becomes for it helps to 'stay the season of a mind'. By turning even the most unlikely stimuli that his confinement offered, the poet kept his mind active without breaking it. The night-prowling cockroach, bats in their blind flights, the priest-like stance of the white-collared crow, the sinister looming of the vulture presiding over the scene of a hanging, are all turned into distancing images through which the mind is released from its immediate restrictions into the larger realities of life outside the prison. Soyinka never abandons his preoccupation with man's universal plight – even in his bitter personal predicament.

The poet himself designates the sequence of poems entitled 'Chimes of Silence' as central to the entire experience represented in *A Shuttle in the Crypt*. The poems show evidence that his facility for economic allusion through imagery remains undiminished. 'Wailing Wall' is typical: In the first stanza parodic echoes of church ritual are intertwined through the priest vulture (later the crow) with the theme of a desecrated death (the inspiration is a hanging). The next stanza continues the parody of a funeral service over which the birds of prey preside, while the image of an un-buried corpse is strongly suggested:

> Crow in white collar, legs
> Of toothpick dearth plunged
> Deep in a salvaged morsel.

By the end of the poem it is not just human corpses which lie buried in a mass grave; even hope is dead:

> Cloud drifts across the Plough
> The share is sunk, and hope
> Buried in soil of darkness.

(The glance at swords and ploughshares is typical in the economy of its suggestiveness.) It is this death of hope that the poem really is about; the hanged corpses supply the stimulus to the poet's imagination.

In 'Last Turning', the poet goes vicariously on the prisoners' last journey. With them he faces the ultimate self-confrontation at the moment of death when 'self encounters self'. With characteristic irony it is light in such circumstances which blinds, and darkness which reveals hidden secrets:

> Pierce the day's elusive blindfold,
> Drink clear-headed of the Night's
> Enlightening potion.

The same irony is evident in the 'black dawn' of 'Mahapralaya' when a man dies to this world and is freed into the next 'to a dark of insight'. Alone he discovers this secret of death:

> a spring is touched by appointed fingers
> and whirlwings fold into the dark
> a glacier mind of all-being
> slows to a last enduring thought
> a deadweight seal of silence sways
> upon the secret – at the wake
> none keep vigil. none

This 'secret' of death has been a preoccupation in earlier works. It is Folasade's 'secret' in 'A First Deathday' (*Idanre and Other Poems*) and it is that for which Professor searched in *The Road*. Prison has brought out the old theme in a new and even more poignant form.

If a man approaches death with a vision that for him is satisfying, if self can confront self without shame, then it is better that he should die with this vision than live to see it tarnished by disillusionment or endure the searing disappointment of seeing his sacrifice violated:

> . . . Kinder this, than a spirit seared
> In violated visions and truths immured.

It may have been kind after all that death came to Christopher Okigbo when and where it did. Thus Soyinka argues himself out of the despair which the death of his friend and fellow-poet might otherwise have bred. The rationalization goes a step beyond the requiem for another friend, Segun Awolowo, in *Idanre*.

When I reviewed *Poems From Prison* in *African Literature Today* No. 4, I observed that the poet's powers of distillation and concentration had survived the mind-bending experience of prison. This larger body of poems from the same experience confirms his survival from his 'live burial'. The tough reasoning, the eye for analogies, the sheer flair for making words work are all still evident. Also apparent is the poet's concern not so much for his personal predicament but for the perverseness in human nature which is so productive of misery.

Taban lo Liyong

Eldred Durosimi Jones

Taban lo Liyong, *Another Nigger Dead,* Heinemann, African Writers Series, London, 1972.

Sometimes, publication notwithstanding, Mr Taban lo Liyong's thoughts remain his private property. 'Batsiary in Sanigraland', one of the prose pieces in *Another Nigger Dead*, still keeps these treasures intact for the author. But in other places, the sacred river bursts the measureless caverns of his mind, and it all comes pouring out. As in the long complaint 'i walked among men' (pp. 55–61) where prose poetry merges into poetic prose and back again to reveal the thoughts of a much wronged 'taban' through marital incommodities, in-law disloyalties, and even university chicanery into sour lonely resignation:

> since i hope for no reward by doing good
> my bough is not a nest for sinners
> please leave me alone
> me and my tranquillity

The sense shines through the passage in spite of the absence of punctuation. Other passages need to be re-read before it becomes clear for example that 'shed' in one context has nothing to do with outbuildings but is Liyongese for 'she'd'. This lack of punctuation combines with puns and adventurous coinages – 'grabious' is a good example – to give even serious passages an air of levity, probably intended, since in the face of some of the lunacies which pass for government in many parts of Africa one has to laugh to keep from crying. And lo Liyong is eventually concerned with with questions like these.

'The filed man' for whom government is a translation of slogans into edicts, in spite of the ludicruous absurdity to which Taban Lo Liyong reduces him, is a potential breeder of misery. He is no less sinister for the comedy with which he is treated. His triumphant achievement of his goal is propounded with an all too familiar empty cocksureness which announces his total obliviousness of the consequences of his edicts

> a functionary reported
> we have at last nationalized POVERTY
> then the filed man laughed the last laugh and said

> didnt i tell you my people
> with good advice from the east
> we can triumph over all our difficulties
> when you follow your leaders
> nothing will go wrong
> our present success shows what can be achieved
> with a little effort
> with the right leadership
> the one leadership

For this kind of ironic statement Liyong's style can be very effective. It catches the vapid rabble-oriented style of the cheap politician while also pointing to the slide into a one party dictatorship. The style does not ring quite so true in every section of the exposition of tragedy in the opening poem which begins:

> bless the african coups
> tragedy now means a thing to us

in spite of the characteristic irony of the opening, and some of the richness suggested by lines like:

> for without hope
> tragedy has never an existence

where 'has never an existence' lacks naturalness, one quality which one would expect in Liyong's generally folksy style.

Something of the character of institutionalized brutality comes out in the purposeful repetitiousness of 'blood iron and trumpets' which ends with the disappearance of all the elements in that recurring phrase – except 'blood alone'. Here form echoes thought, and the final construct stands indissoluble.

Liyong's style is one of accumulation. It is paratactical in a way that is reminiscent of the narrative and poetic styles of many African Languages. Ideas, sometimes straight, sometimes ironic, humorous, serious, parallel, contrasting are massed together with a studied carelessness to produce a prickly, jumpy effect. The wheat and the tares are allowed to grow together in a reflection perhaps of the state of this imperfect world. But need the task of sorting them one from the other be made more difficult for the reader by an absence of punctuation? For the eye alone the poetry seems to flow, but for everything else this lack of punctuation slows down comprehension.

Mbella Sonne Dipoko

Eldred Durosimi Jones

Mbella Sonne Dipoko, *Black and White in Love*, Heinemann, African Writers Series, London, 1972

Black and White in Love is an effort at self-confession where confession in no way implies contrition; self-exposure is perhaps a better phrase. There is no doubt about the poet's beliefs; declarations of his state, his purpose, and his ideals confront us everywhere:

> I am black
> And a hippy
> And I sing

In answer to his father's pardonable bewilderment as to what his son could be doing in Europe, his answer is frank and clear:

> Just being myself, daddy,
> Kissing across the colourline.

There is abundant testimony in the poems to this type of activity – in poems to 'B' to 'H', M.C., not to mention more casual companions. Indeed 'kissing across the colourline' is what the title poem 'Black and White in Love' is all about, and the poems speak of this occupation rather as if it was some kind of black man's burden fraught with agony –

> the strain known
> In our cruel world
> Only to those who have ever loved
> One who is not their own colour.

Of this sort of statement the poems are full, and one can believe in the agony or not as he chooses; take the poet at his own valuation or beg leave to doubt at will, for these feelings are subjective to the poet.

However the persistence with which the poems talk of other matters – the *struggle* against oppression (black and white), the constant suggestions of the risk the poet runs of savage victimization, and of his unflinching determination to carry on the liberation struggle regardless of consequences make one search for credentials. The poet after all is in danger of his life –

> What does it matter
> If some of us are murdered(?)

One looks for credentials to justify the implied authority and of lines like:

> The class struggle is real indeed
> And I have comrades beyond the colourline
> And there are black oppressors who need
>   interminable elegies of the past;
> And there are black oppressed and exploited who
>   need the future
> I stand by the latter against the former.

There is little in the poems to back these claims. And it is legitimate, I suggest, to expect such backing from poems which are so frankly anti-iographical and so explicit. (No other African poet is so engagingly free with the first personal pronoun.) The poet is doing his own thing. He is seen 'carrying my bag of manuscripts and newspapers' (for the former of which occasionally a cheque arrives from Heinemann), he makes love in the open air, outsmarts trusting capitalists and policemen, lives off his friends and writes about all this. What, one is tempted to inquire has all this to do with the revolution that is so persistently invoked?

But the poet is honest, and sometimes reveals that he himself sees through his own rationalizations – as in this passage from the title poem:

> And do you still remember how
> In the shadows of the sierras
> I used to talk to you
> Of the glory of the struggle
> For national liberation
> And you just sitting there
> And it not occurring to you
> What a fool I was
> Spending my time
> Making love
> In the underground
> And fighting my revolutions
> In the head?

For such frankness one can forgive the poet much that would otherwise have been pretentious, but even brotherly love must have bounds and one must require more justification for this representation of the poet as a saviour in peril of his life. Is being an 'outlaw' enough? Or is

> Burning incense and reading the Koran
> By candle-light

in a locked loo in the Latin Quarter a particularly revolutionary act?

The defence for looking so much at the content of these poems is that they are very close to prose – a style which admittedly suits the intention of frank revelation admirably. Occasionally nevertheless the poet presents **179** individual ideas in a strikingly poetic way. Like the cynical brutality of his friend D who had returned

> with so many souvenirs of his safari
> Across the kindness of my black people.

He succeeds in portraying the persistence of basic human nature in spite of changes in man's style of living in:

> The causes remain the same
> The rituals have only gone into trenches
> And sacrificial blood flows in pipe-lines

There is a wealth of suggestiveness – long, agonizing, debilitating, pointless waiting in the single line

> For days have grown beards.

This line is, however, immediately succeeded, indeed paralleled, by a far less striking one:

> And nights have become lonesome.

The distance between the two lines suggests the difference in poetic quality that can be encountered in this poet's verse.

One of the best examples of a sustained use of imagery, striking in its aptness, is from the poem 'The Night'. It has the dry crackling quality of the imagery of Eliot:

> We are not waiting
> For the alarm clock
> Which will ring no more
> Its spring being cut
> And someone has played the clockbird's dirge
> It lies dead
> Under the window
> Where the blood-stained feathers will soon be made into a pillow
> (But not by us)

This to me is Dipoko at his best – forging poetry out of the materials of the hour.

These poems are at their liveliest and best when they depict a picaresque adventurer letting life take him along; in this light they are revealing informative, and eminently readable. As manifestoes of a revolutionary, well, that is another matter altogether.

Chinua Achebe

Eldred Durosimi Jones

Chinua Achebe, *Beware Soul Brother*, Heinemann, African
Writers Series, London, 1972.

Out of all proportion to their size but in due reflection of their grim intensity
it is the 'Poems about War' above all the other groups in this collection
that leave the deepest impression on the mind. All the poems however
share the quality of economy. Their immediate meaning is clear enough
but they go beyond clarity and bring associations beyond their immediate
literal scope.

In 'Refugee Mother and Child' the picture of emaciated children is grim
in a physical way; but it is the fruitlessness of a mother's loving care which
burns deep into our consciousness as she combs and parts the hair on the
head of her starving child, hair which by its very growing mocks life itself.
How well Achebe represents the idea:

> In another life this
> would have been a little daily
> act of no consequence before his
> breakfast and school; now she
> did it like putting flowers
> on a tiny grave.

The evocation of 'school' and 'breakfast' now as distant as 'another life' in
proximity with the suggestions of death and of loving but futile floral
tributes illustrates the control and the economy which is a common quality
of the poems in *Beware Soul Brother*. The control is equally in the selection of details and in the language in which they are presented. A child is
also at the centre of the succeeding poem 'Christmas in Biafra'. For the
famine-stricken child, the manger scene means nothing. His death-in-life
is a complete travesty of the meaning of Christmas, and this is highlighted
by the contrasting picture of the baby in the manger:

> Jesus plump wise-looking and rose-cheeked

Not all the poems are about war, but the same eye quick to spot the
irony of things is present throughout. Resurrection may bring joy to some,
but not to every one:

> Certainly that keen-eyed
> subordinate who had moved up

181

to his table at the office, for
him resurrection is an awful
embarrassment.

There is humour here of a grim kind. More than once Achebe calls up a
wan smile at ironies like those evoked by the fate of the twice killed man of
Ogbaku in 'Lazarus'.

Like his Igbo people Achebe is always conscious of 'the duality of things'.
The Americans hanged war criminals after the last world war and now find
themselves looking askance at their own Vietnam 'heroes'. Justice comes
out rather tarnished from 'An "if" of History':

Had Hitler won,
Vidkun Quisling would have kept
His job as Prime Minister
of Norway. . . .

As Shakespeare's Lear put it 'handy dandy which is the justice, which is
the thief?'

The casual way in which man unleashes holocausts upon himself is well
imagined by the oil drill in '1966'; the drill casually set in motion bores
artesian wells of blood in an act which, recalling the first failure of Adam
and Eve, suggests man's chronic proneness to self-defeat. All this is
economically suggested; one suggestion reinforcing another without
duplicating it:

a diamond-tipped
drillpoint crept closer
to residual chaos to
rare artesian hatred
that once squirted warm
blood in God's face
confirming His first
disappointment in Eden.

Achebe uses punctuation marks sparingly. He avoids, however, the total
renunciation of these guides to understanding as some modern poets have
done and communicated his urgent meanings readily.

The collection is an immense achievement. The Biafran War lost as a
remarkable poet – Okigbo; it has given us a new assured poetic voice –
Achebe.

Index

184

185

Lightning Source UK Ltd.
Milton Keynes UK
UKHW021958281122
413003UK00012B/714